Volume 6

I0130644

PUBLIC HOUSING IN EUROPE AND AMERICA

PUBLIC HOUSING IN EUROPE AND AMERICA

Edited by
J. S. FUERST

Routledge
Taylor & Francis Group

LONDON AND NEW YORK

First published in 1974 by Croom Helm Ltd

This edition first published in 2021
by Routledge
2 Park Square, Milton Park, Abingdon, Oxon OX14 4RN

and by Routledge
52 Vanderbilt Avenue, New York, NY 10017

Routledge is an imprint of the Taylor & Francis Group, an informa business

© 1974 Croom Helm Ltd

British Library Cataloguing in Publication Data
A catalogue record for this book is available from the British Library

ISBN: 978-0-367-64519-9 (Set)
ISBN: 978-1-00-313856-3 (Set) (ebk)
ISBN: 978-0-367-67895-1 (Volume 6) (hbk)
ISBN: 978-0-367-67901-9 (pbk)
ISBN: 978-1-00-313329-2 (Volume 6) (ebk)

Publisher's Note
The publisher has gone to great lengths to ensure the quality of this reprint but points out that some imperfections in the original copies may be apparent.

Disclaimer
The publisher has made every effort to trace copyright holders and would welcome correspondence from those they have been unable to trace.

Public Housing in
Europe and America

Edited by J. S. FUERST

CROOM HELM LONDON

First published 1974
© 1974 by Croom Helm Ltd

Croom Helm Ltd, 2–10 St John's Road, London SW11

ISBN 0 85664-053-0

Printed in Great Britain
by Ebenezer Baylis & Son Ltd
The Trinity Press, Worcester, and London
Bound by G. & J. Kitcat Ltd, London

Contents

Foreword

It has been estimated that man, in the temperate zones, spends about 80 per cent of his lifetime in relatively large containers—in residential and non-residential structures. It is mainly in these containers that he performs the various functions that fill his life space—work, play, education, religion, sleep, etc. Moreover, his containers, primarily his housing, provide him with security—protection against inclement weather, ravages of nature and depredations of fellow men. Yet throughout the world, in the economically advanced as well as in the developing areas, large housing deficits are to be found, both quantitatively and qualitatively. Especially is this true for low and moderate income groups—which include the preponderant proportion of the population in the less developed nations. This is the case, however, even in the United States, the most affluent of all nations.

The economically advanced countries have, for more than a century in some instances (England, France, Germany, Denmark and Sweden), been attempting to improve the situation for the ill-housed by various forms of government intervention, direct and indirect. In the United States, possessed with its frontier traditions of self-reliance, independence, and resistance to the 'welfare state', government did not begin to play a significant role in attempting to improve the housing of its poor until the depression of the 1930s. Although successive housing enactments in the USA have increasingly promised much, relatively little has been accomplished through government action on behalf of the ill-housed. Moreover, as has become increasingly clear, what has been done in respect of public housing in the United States has ranged from the inadequate to the disastrous.

Mr Fuerst in this volume presents a comprehensive review of social housing programmes in Europe and in the United States. It is an informative work for everybody throughout the world interested in social housing, and 'must' reading for all those in the United States concerned with finding new directions away from the public housing morass into which this nation has blundered.

Philip M. Hauser
University of Chicago

Preface

I have been associated with public housing since 1946. At that time, there were already great difficulties in the way of the programme: hostile local communities; antagonistic real estate and banking groups; and, of course, the ever present racial prejudice with which we had to contend. Nevertheless, the programme in Chicago, New York, Pittsburgh, Baltimore, and many more cities hobbled along under a group of well-meaning, and in many cases able, executive directors and commissioners. By 1955, however, the number of good authorities dwindled to a handful, and the programme was on its way to becoming all-black, segregated, high-rise, and poverty-oriented with the seeds of its ultimate destruction evident.

Around this time my active participation in the programme was lessened because I went into private business where I remained for some fifteen years. During this period I continued to be deeply interested in public housing generally, and specifically in programmes in New York, Puerto Rico and Pittsburgh, where the programme was still vital, though winding down and I also followed the programmes in many other countries. I visited Europe, Israel, Puerto Rico to evaluate the programmes in action, and I observed how mistakes that we in the United States had made were frequently being avoided in Europe. Where basic mistakes were made, they were more often rectified because there was less built-in antagonism to public enterprise. It has always seemed to me that we in the United States have been extremely parochial about utilising the contributions of other countries, at least in our public enterprises if not our private ones. We report their activities in our periodicals or news media, but we utilise their techniques infrequently.

In providing housing for the low-moderate income groups this was particularly true. It seemed to me indispensable, therefore, if housing of the best sort were to be provided for low and moderate income workers, that some compilation be made of the significant contributions of each country to social housing programmes. Parts of the United States had developed some interesting techniques, certainly New York City and Puerto Rico; West Germany had a fine union housing programme; Israel and Great Britain both had extensive

public housing programmes; France and USSR had extensive industrialised systems housing programmes; and Israel had a big low-
income ownership programme.

The book covers housing in ten countries, but it also tells much
about the nature and approach of different nations to their housing
problems. Each of the articles bears the imprint of national characteristics and indicates how these differences affect the housing
programme. What is most significant, despite the political divergen-
cies, is the similar attitudes and programmes in all the European
countries, and Israel, where government responsibility for housing is
an accepted fact.

I was encouraged by my friend, John Ducey, formerly associated
with me at the Chicago Housing Authority and later at Loyola
University, to publish these findings, which I did, choosing from
each country the particular contribution which seemed to be
pre-eminent. In fact, since I became associated with Loyola
University in 1967, I have received great encouragement from the
Urban Studies Department, notably Michael Schiltz. Likewise I
want to thank Harry Fialkin of the New York City Housing
Authority for the great assistance he provided with the material on
the early public housing programme and the New York City
operation.

The Hungarian article was obtained through the offices of my good
friends, Chicago architects John Macsai and Al Hedvige, to whom I
am most grateful. While in Hungary they arranged a meeting with
Mr Gaspar, an eminent Hungarian architect, who agreed to write
the article.

I also want to express my appreciation to Joseph Wandel of
Loyola University, to Jean Fondrevais of the French consulate, and
to Dr and Mrs Gosta Ahlstrom for their help with the German,
French, Swedish and Danish translations.

I want to offer thanks to my son, Dan, who worked over the book,
offering valuable editorial help and suggestions; to my daughter,
Ruth, for her helpful suggestions; and to my secretaries Janet
Struble and Mary Schiltz who handled the typing, seeing me through
all the revisions with good grace and tolerance. But above all I owe
a debt impossible to pay to my wife, Dorothy, who worried and
suffered with me through the research, travel and writing, with
encouragement and personal sacrifices.

Finally, the book would never have seen print had I not had the constant help and support of my friend, Roy Porter, who spent many hours helping me through the thicket of publication.

The book is not an academic exercise. It is written with the sincere hope that all countries can benefit by examining the public housing contributions of others, including those that succeeded, and also those errors that were made as solutions evolved. Out of such richness, all nations can find new methods for improving and strengthening their social housing programmes.

Chapter 1   Review of Social Housing in the World

J. S. FUERST

Providing adequate housing for people is one of the great problems in the world today. In many places it is the lack of adequate places to live combined with the lack of jobs that is causing the desperation, riots and general social upheaval characteristic of life in even the most advanced countries.

According to classical economic theory, it was assumed that a free market regulated by the price mechanism would provide all the housing that was needed. Private builders supported this concept, arguing that the less government involvement the more opportunity for freedom of choice; but the actual motivation was less complicated: *laissez faire* meant more profit. Free market theory economists continue to assert that purchase price and rent as regulatory devices maximise production and are conducive to a greater distributive justice than arbitrary decisions effecting the market made by deliberative bodies.

Housing conditions of blue-collar and white-collar workers in Western Europe and the USA make it clear that private building under a free market mechanism has not provided adequately for these groups. Building construction, a most cyclical affair depending upon the economic climate, serves only a part of the population and leaves large groups of families untouched. Poorer families would ultimately be housed, according to classical theory, as well-to-do families moved out of their housing to new buildings and the older housing filtered down to the poorer sections of the community. While this happened to some degree, the houses were frequently in a shoddy state when the lower income groups moved into them.

Since family size in the lower end of the income curve was larger than at the upper end, the housing was not suitable for many of the poorer families. Actually with land prices out of control, with building labour protecting its interests and with costs rocketing, private enterprise construction of new housing at a price within the means of low or moderate wage-earners was impossible. Government intervention therefore became axiomatic and by 1970 the only questions remaining in most Western nations were how much housing should be provided by government aid, of what kind, at what level, where would the money come from specifically, and who would control it?

Before 1900 government took little responsibility for housing but since the turn of the century it has played varying roles in different nations. In many instances there was an unrelenting struggle carried on by banks, landowners and building industries to keep government out of housing. They argued that government intervention could be salutary in the beginning but then would only lead to disaster in the form of paternalism, socialism and finally authoritarianism.

Through writers such as Dickens, Ruskin and Zola society was made more consciously aware of its moral responsibilities and the necessity of government intervention was dimly recognised. Years went by, however, before the problems these reformers described were recognised in any meaningful way by governments. Nevertheless, in the late 1800s housing legislation was passed; mostly of a protective nature, being designed to inhibit the worst type of slum housing and health conditions. Still, in most of the Western European countries and in the USA, little was done actually to provide public housing. Although a few reformers or socialists saw government assistance as a means of providing housing for the masses at this time, most of them saw self-help through co-operatives or union-sponsored housing as the answer. They objected to government intervention almost as much as the industrialists.

England, in 1857, enacted a Labouring Classes Lodging Act and in 1867 France enacted a Societies' Act to enable the building of co-operatives but neither Act provided any substantial amount of building by or for workers. In Germany, with its strong trade union movement, and in Sweden the workers' organisations made somewhat more headway and similarly such movements occurred in Switzerland, Austria and Holland.

The co-operative movement had its beginnings in 1869 in Denmark, 1870 in Sweden and 1889 in Germany. In general the co-operative movement had an extra quality about it beyond the provision of homes for those needing them. Correspondingly, in nations where co-operative movements have begun and where such commitments were lacking, for whatever reason, co-operatives have enjoyed little real success, for example, in the USA where the co-operative movement never really took hold. On the other hand in many other countries, the movement has included workers' co-operatives formed around occupational groups such as teachers, civil servants, railroad employees and postal workers.

Apart from union or co-operative housing operations, some workers' housing was provided by philanthropists or in conjunction with an employment scheme, but no substantial inroads into the housing needs of workers were made by this method.

While the British were among the earliest to have enacted protective legislation against harmful housing conditions, it was not until late in the nineteenth century that they turned to non-profit housing to any degree. Essentially, their first provision was local government housing for the aged, the infirm and fatherless families who were unable to obtain housing for themselves. While this programme did not grow rapidly, by the 1930s it was the largest of its kind in the world.

During the depression of the 1930s attempts were made to build more government and non-profit housing. Sweden saw some growth at this time. Germany experienced a growth in union and co-operative housing, but they were brought to a halt by the policies of National Socialism which placed no priority on housing at all. France showed little development and had one of the poorest records up to the end of the Second World War. The USSR had apparently too many other priorities to concern itself much with housing. The USA started to provide limited government funds in an attempt to bring the building industry out of a slump, and at the same time clear slums and build low-rent housing. The programme was activated in 1935 and by 1941, when the USA entered the Second World War, a small amount of housing had been constructed but virtually no more was begun until after the war.

After the Second World War most of the countries of Western Europe, devastated by depression and war, were no longer willing to accept the word of their 'men of affairs' that private enterprise should go it alone as far as housing was concerned. An intensive programme of government aid to housing was begun in the alternative forms of municipal housing, governmental housing, housing co-operatives, union housing, subsidies to individuals and municipalities and provision of housing for special groups.

West Germany, economically and politically an amalgam of

capitalism and socialism, developed a strong housing programme in both the private and co-operative sector. In the co-operative sector, union-sponsored housing was an important component and catalytic agent. Germany has made a most successful attempt to provide a high level of housing within a limited free market operation. Nevertheless, with a long history in workers' organisation, it is not surprising that the unions have one of the strongest housing programmes in the world, and Germany has attempted to shape rather than merely regulate the planning and housing growth of its cities. In this connection, Germany did not follow the path of national or local provision of housing as in Britain, or even France. Government loans and tax concessions operated through non-governmental operations. The lower half of the population could not hope to obtain housing in the private market. Hence, at least one-third of German housing is channelled through the non-profit groups, most notably the co-operatives and the union organisations and Neue Heimat, the union-sponsored programme, particularly. Through the imaginative use of taxation and subsidies and through the extensive use of these co-operatives and unions, Germany has maintained a free market, fostered owner-occupation where possible and provided much-needed social housing. Today, Germany has one of the highest rates of total building per 1,000 population; one of the lowest rates of persons per room, and one of the highest dwelling counts per population in Europe and the USA. The special contribution West Germany has made to world non-profit housing is in the expertise of its union-organised housing programme.

Similarly, Denmark, Sweden and Israel, as well as Germany, developed significant amounts of housing under union auspices, following the Second World War, with German and Israeli workers' organisations having the most widespread operations. In Israel, Histradrut, the labour organisation which operates a housing programme, also provides a full-scale welfare programme and has a very strong political arm.

Denmark and Sweden, with strong co-operative strains, powerful workers' parties and less involvement with the USA and the USSR chose different paths. This was especially true of Sweden with no large post-war debt nor devastation to overcome. As a result both the union and the co-operative movement developed strongly in Sweden and within five years of the end of the war, a full-scale housing programme blossomed. It was divided among the publicly-financed, the co-operative with public assistance and the privately-operated organisations. Housing was constructed within the framework of government plans and today almost 90 per cent of the housing in Sweden is underwritten by the government.

Sweden leads the world in dwelling units per population, amenities per dwelling unit, proportion of units built after 1948, units of new housing constructed per 1,000 population and provision of total planning for the communities. Nevertheless, even with this record, Sweden has a long waiting list for apartments which is only decreasing today because of unemployment. Sweden realised the need for government help after the building industry collapsed and a deep depression set in after the Second World War. Thereafter, Sweden placed itself in the top rung of countries in terms of government expenditure for residential purposes as a proportion of GNP; and as a result Sweden has the lowest proportion of strictly private construction outside the Eastern bloc countries. Essentially, co-operatives, with good assistance from the unions, have been used to institute the housing programme in Sweden; municipal housing, although it figures more prominently than in Germany, Denmark or Holland, has not played a major role in Sweden's programme.

Denmark believes the co-operative movement to be the most important non-profit method of providing housing for the lower income groups of the community. They believe, also, that government should control housing and land planning; and land controls exercised by Copenhagen are among the most stringent in the West. The combination of intensive building and industrialisation and extensive use of government finance and planning, supplemented by a strong co-operative movement, has made Denmark one of the leaders in housing per capita and in gross national product per capita.

The Netherlands has had an unusually high population growth and one of the highest densities in the West. Yet it is a country where a high degree of economic and social development has combined with a growing birth rate and rapid growth in family size. At the same time, this country has met its housing commitments to a remarkable degree with a large number of urban centres, rather than encouraging concentration in a single conurbation, a relatively low amount of mobility and a firm control of land by the state. Their non-profit housing provision has been mostly through co-operatives, though they do possess some municipal housing.

An important contribution of the Dutch to urban housing is their special projects for problem families. The problem is a focal point for social housing programmes world-wide, although most countries do not provide special housing for 'hard core' social-problem families. The Netherlands has experimented with a series of programmes and housing projects for this type of family and provides six projects where work has been going on for twenty years.

Great Britain, after Switzerland, affords the greatest degree of local autonomy among the European nations. Council housing in Great Britain has been developed into the largest local authority housing programme in the world. In some areas, such as Scotland, council housing constitutes almost one-half of all housing built. At the present time, because of the controls on rent in the private sector, practically no rental housing is built by private entrepreneurs and the field is left to local authorities. The fact that there must be council housing for those who cannot afford to buy housing is recognised even by the Conservative government. As the price of housing rockets, fewer and fewer families can afford to purchase homes and correspondingly more families need to have council housing. The attitude is reflected in the policy of building 'new towns' which is an important development in Britain.

Israel has even more public housing proportionately than Great Britain but its development has necessarily been different. Israel assumed statehood in 1948 and with this came a huge influx of immigrants who had to be housed. Because of the socialist background of its leaders, many of whom had been raised in the social democratic parties of Western Europe, the needs of the people were met from the outset by large-scale national governmental provision of housing. One of the most important differences between Israel and most other countries was the recognition of the immediate need to disperse people throughout the country. While other countries recognise this necessity, because they are not dealing with as large a proportion of immigrants, their options are not as great. The Israeli new-town development, widely dispersed throughout the country, is their greatest housing contribution. Moreover, the large number of immigrants to Israel from Middle Europe with strong working-class and co-operative backgrounds made possible one of the more important union housing programmes in the world; and as a result of the diversity of origin of Israel's population the integration of immigrants became a significant focus of the Israeli programme.

France at the end of the Second World War suffered from an enormously disadvantaged housing situation along with a strongly individualistic centralised political tradition. A slow starter after the war, France laboured to re-establish itself economically, politically and psychologically as an important member of the European family of nations. Foreign affairs came first and housing was largely ignored. Rent controls were retained by the government out of fear they might have had difficulty surviving in office without them rather than to protect the tenants with low incomes. As a result, there was little private rented housing for many years after the war and not a great deal of public housing. Part of this was due to the low population growth in France. In general, housing conditions in France were poorer than other European countries particularly in the number of rooms per person, bathroom facilities per dwelling and age of housing. Around 1950, however, France accelerated its programme and, with increased industrialisation and a growing population, devoted a larger portion of its national income to housing than hitherto. Because of the emphasis on the individual, a special form of public housing was initiated, a type of quasi-public corporation with some of the legal characteristics of private companies but many of the properties of public bodies. They were under the control of the municipality as well as national government, with the national government regulating housing expenditure, income limits, and rent to be charged. Control over banking by the government is tight and the channels through which investments are made in the housing field are within its sphere. The government attempts to allow a free market; but they use several types of taxation as well as legislative restrictions to try to curb speculation, though not always successfully. They have strict land and technical building controls and seem determined, moreover, to provide a significant amount of housing for a large segment of the population including the lowest income groups.

Eastern Europe illustrates what can be done with government ownership of housing and some of the difficulties, as well as the advantages, of complete government control. Perhaps most surprising to Western European and American observers is the extent to which the USSR and Hungary, to mention only two countries, continue to permit private ownership of housing. In rural areas private ownership remains characteristic, though where new towns are built homes are usually government owned. A reason for the large number of rural private homes is the fact that prefabrication has not yet reached into the countryside to the degree that it has in the cities. Also many of the homes are old and the state encourages private ownership because it relieves some of the pressure for immediate state building. However, even in new construction, there is some private building of single family homes; and a great push towards co-operatives, a modified form of private ownership. In many communities professional and upper civil-service families, as well as the managerial cliques, tend to buy into co-operatives, with the state's encouragement.

One of the important differences between East and West is the degree of control exercised by the government, though governments in the West may greatly influence the amount of housing built through indirect controls. In the USSR, however, up to 1954, little emphasis was placed on housing and although the population grew and in some new towns grew considerably, the government was able to survive without adding significantly to the housing stock. Nevertheless, since this time, they have accounted for almost half the housing produced in Europe. However, their dwellings are small and rooms per dwelling very limited. But, as in Israel, this has been changing and in very recent years, the size and variety of rooms and apartments has been improving. As part of their overall plan, they have been experimenting on factory-built housing and are the biggest users of industrialised housing in the world. Among other things this means that many of the units are small in size, uniform in shape and are grouped in large projects with populations as high as 6,000 to 10,000; the primary objective is quantity rather than quality.

Hungary is a good example of a satellite country with very poor housing conditions after the war. Only a quarter of the people had piped water in their dwellings and the number of persons per room was one of the highest in Europe. During the last ten years an improved rate of industrialisation has been accompanied by a much greater emphasis on housing. The question of private ownership is still present and Hungary has allowed large numbers of the population to remain in their own homes, easing the immediate problem of building for all. As in Soviet Russia, there is emphasis upon co-operatives in new building. Likewise, the situation in Hungary exemplifies the conflict between those who wish to live in older areas in rehabilitated housing and those who wish to live in the new housing in outlying areas which the state is building. Hungary manifests the great problems of starting a full-scale building programme, particularly in Budapest where there has been a significant attempt to stop the flow of immigration into the city by limiting housing for rural immigrants. In a sense, this is the same objective of new-town programmes in Britain, Israel and Sweden, but in Hungary, because of the great housing need, relatively low degree of development and greater ease of government control, it becomes more a question of coercion and less of promotion to achieve the end.

A recent entry into a public housing programme is Spain. It may be noted that despite the orientation of the conservative government towards private enterprise and the relatively low income taxation, there has been large-scale government production of housing during the past ten years. Because of the autocratic nature of the government there are fewer difficulties in the way than in the USA or in Britain. Well over 50 per cent of the housing constructed has been government 'social housing'. All over Spain housing is being constructed with government aids of one type or another; co-operatives are being built, as are housing projects for government railroad workers and other occupational groups and large blocks of national government housing. The volume of building is substantial, representing in total, about nine units per year for every 1,000 in the population, an enormous increase over their record ten years ago. The largest blocks are being built in the outlying areas. In such places as Barcelona and Madrid where there are enormous concentrations of high rise blocks, many of these are quite monotonous in design, lacking in amenities and have a relatively small number of rooms per apartment compared with the size of family. On the other hand, there are marked improvements in the housing built in recent years, both in size and in design.

The United States has one of the highest amounts of living space and bath facilities per capita. Moreover, an average worker can buy a home with a smaller percentage of his salary than workers in other countries. Nevertheless, with more deteriorating housing, judging by the 1960 census (since the 1970 census elected not to carry the measure) and more families in 'slum' areas than in many of the countries of Europe, the US government takes little real responsibility for housing. Federal laws are full of provisions for public housing, for co-operative housing, for university housing, for non-profit and union-sponsored housing and for varieties of subsidies; yet only a few of these schemes have come to fruition. As a result, new housing built in any quantity is directed at the middle and upper income segments of the population and the percentage of non-profit housing to total housing is lower than any of the Western European countries despite the apparent need for such housing in the USA. One major difference between the USA and the other countries is that despite the great need among the lower- and middle-income population there is not, in great contrast for example to Britain, any hue and cry in the localities, except among blacks and other minority groups. Most ask for more money but not for more housing.

The fundamental premise of this book is that housing cannot and will not be produced in the future without substantial aid from governments in one form or another. The purpose of the book is to examine various methods employed in different countries in the effort to improve the housing stock, emphasising the particular expertise employed, in producing housing and in meeting housing need.

Chapter 2   How Britain Builds Houses

TERENCE BENDIXSON

The concept that communities have the responsibility to provide housing for low-income families is a firmly established tradition in Great Britain. As far back as the Middle Ages the landed gentry built alms houses for the poor, some of which are still to be found in a number of villages. The resulting rows of gabled cottages were an answer to the Christian command to love thy neighbour as thyself and an insurance against the fires of hell. They are also among the finest examples of small-scale architecture in Europe.

The modern idea of public housing in Great Britain gained impetus during the First World War. A wartime housing shortage led central government to make grants available to local authorities that were responsible for financing and promoting the building of houses for working-class families in need. The practice of building houses with public funds has continued in one way or another in Great Britain ever since.

The result is that, according to the 1966 census, of 17·4 million homes in Britain, 8·1 million were privately owned, 3·4 million were owned and rented out by private landlords and 4·9 million were owned and rented out by local authorities and New Towns. Other forms of tenure accounted for the remainder. In Greater London (population 7·7 million) the stock of 2·2 million houses was composed of 1 million privately owned homes, 681,000 rented from private landlords and 551,000 rented from councils. About 200,000 council houses are now owned and managed by the Greater London Council (GLC), which is the regional authority for the city, and the rest by the London borough councils.

Public housing in Britain is subsidised in three ways:

(1) The central government helps local authorities to pay the loan charges on borrowed capital and the grant from the government is

calculated to cover the difference between 4 per cent interest level and current bank rates.

(2) Local authorities use rent profits from houses already built, e.g. in 1930 for £750, to reduce rents on new houses built for about £9,000 today.

(3) Local councils take a given amount of money from property taxes and shift the money to housing accounts. In this way members of a community help to subsidise poorer neighbours, provided that the municipal boundaries do not separate rich and poor.

Current practice, however, is to try to reduce the amount of subsidy in council housing. In fact, between 1951 and 1967, Exchequer subsidies dropped from 25 to 18 per cent of local authority housing incomes, and rate subsidies dropped from 13 to 8 per cent. The difference was made up by rent increases.

In general, Britain's housing policies came under scrutiny in the 1960s, creating a feeling that changes would be made. Many changes did in point of fact take place in the Housing Finance Act of 1972 which required the local councils to charge fair (higher) rents and operate with a system of rent rebates for the poorer. Individual councils have been placed in a kind of financial strait-jacket with little freedom to determine their own rent policies. Under this same Act, as of April 1, 1973, a tenant of a private landlord may be able to claim from the local authority a 'rent allowance' if the 'fair' rent he is being charged is beyond his means. An extreme view is that the country should go over completely to a system of income supports that would enable anyone, however poor, to pay the market rent for an adequate home irrespective of whether it is owned by a private or municipal landlord. This may be what the future holds, but such ideas were unacceptable when existing policies were formulated and the chosen instrument for improving the domestic conditions of the poor has long been the building of houses.

Furthermore, there are reasons for believing that municipal housing can play a vital role at any time. The real issue is not whether subsidised homes should be built for people in need, but how many and for whom should they be built.

The results of Britain's current housing policies are reflected in the country's annual output of houses and flats, increasing at the annual rate of between 425,000 (1968) and 363,000 (1970 total). In 1970 the total was split almost in half with 174,000 homes being built for sale and 189,000 for letting by local authorities.

However, this national balance conceals local differences, in particular the dominant role of local authorities in rebuilding worn out old neighbourhoods in the great cities, and the equally dominant role of private builders on virgin unused land on the fringes of and beyond the conurbations.

Thus, in Greater London, in 1971, the local councils built 22,400 homes while private firms completed 8,400. But to the south of the capital, in green and open counties such as Surrey and Sussex, the ratio for the same period was 7,334 council to 15,552 private.

Nor do the Greater London figures tell the complete story, for in some of the tightly-packed inner areas of London, constructed in the eighteenth and nineteenth centuries, the role of the public authorities is even more dominant. The borough of Islington, to the north of the ancient walled City of London, is a case in point. In 1971, the council completed 581 new homes while private builders finished only 29.

What this points to is that the cost of redeveloping the old inner areas of London is so great, in poor neighbourhoods, that only public authorities are capable of assuming the responsibility of providing accommodation for poorer families. Using their powers of compulsory purchase, local councils need pay only the site value of old houses certified as medically unfit to live in. But if they buy adequate housing nearby, in order to get sites of suitable shape for redevelopment, they have to pay market prices for them. Until recently councils hardly ever resold such sites but now policy on this is changing. In some cases compulsorily acquired land is being sold to help a non-profit housing organisation and the GLC is beginning to sell sites adjacent to property on which it is building to private builders in order to increase the social diversity of neighbourhoods. Moreover, GLC is beginning to build houses specifically for resale at a discount off the market value. This is the subject of much political argument and it is recognised that the future of this programme depends upon which political party is in power after the April 1973 local government elections.

This is but one example of the new thinking in British housing policy and is a result of the political dialogue between the Labour and Conservative parties. Another innovation is the practice of buying handsome and historically interesting old buildings, modernising them where necessary at considerable expense and then letting them out at economic rents. As a result of this approach the children of two ex-Cabinet ministers are living in flats rented at market rates from the GLC in a new estate beside the Thames. The flats have been constructed in an old rum warehouse, at Deptford, that has been reconditioned in the course of the redevelopment of an old naval dockyard. At places still under construction, such as the riverside new town of Thamesmead, which will house 45,000, the hope is that a marina and other amenities will attract speculative house-builders and that one-third of the homes in the town will be for sale. This is a far cry from the practice of the 1930s when the Becontree estate was built as a solid slab of rented council houses next to Ford's at Dagenham.

The powers that local authorities have to buy property compulsorily also enable them to buy and clear houses in order to make way for schools, parks and roads as well as to build new homes. Consequently, in 1969, the GLC allocated 400 of its vacant tenancies to families displaced by roads. Schemes for schools required another 675 families to be rehoused and park requirements 275 more.

Failing successful negotiations, court orders can be served on the owners of slums to oblige them to make improvements. In either case the local authority will contribute to the cost of new bathrooms, lavatories and kitchens. If this also fails to provide results, the authority can get the work done itself and seek to recover the costs, or take over and manage such a building, or buy it compulsorily.

A measure of the circumstances which make such drastic powers necessary is provided by the figures of overcrowding and ill-equipped homes in London. The 1966 census revealed that about 635,000 families in London, or approximately one in four, were sharing houses, 388,000 dwellings had no bath, and 247,000 had no indoor toilet.

Thus, it should be apparent that the difficulties of maintaining the domestic arrangements of a city of nearly eight million are immense. It is a complexity multiplied by centuries of building and rebuilding, by changes in jobs, innovations in transport and rising expectations. In this urban world, the importance of the Greater London Council, the elected authority set up in 1965 with responsibilities for land planning, housing and major highways throughout the 610 square miles of the capital and parts of its surrounding green belt, cannot be exaggerated. Furthermore, when the GLC assumed the management of London's red buses and subways in 1970, it was placed in an ideal position to co-ordinate the major public services that Londoners require.

In the housing field, the GLC already owns about 200,000 houses and flats spread throughout the urban area. These vary from modest two-storey houses with gardens in the outer suburbs to blocks of flats just across the Thames from the Houses of Parliament.

This huge conglomeration of housing enabled the Council to offer homes to 13,000 families in 1971. Nearly 5,000 of the lettings were newly built, 1,300 were conversions or modernisations of older council property, and 6,200 were the result of tenancies falling vacant.

In addition, the GLC is currently co-operating with local councils in town expansion projects in thirty country towns in other parts of England. The objective of this is to provide more people with the opportunity to escape the grip of the Great Wen and so create more room for those left behind. An office has been opened to assist industrialists in their move to the same towns in order to ensure that people going to the country do not have to commute back to the city.

A total of 38,000 (June 1969) country homes have been built in this manner since 1954 while another 86,000 are planned. Factories covering 18 million square feet have been established by firms moving from London to twenty of the towns. Currently the GLC is spending £13·7 millions a year in this way in order to assist the London community. This plan for action is structured so that the GLC does not receive a penny back in property taxes although there can be little doubt that the result will be a more healthy and prosperous community.

Similar emergency assistance projects, albeit on a larger scale and called New Towns, are being promoted by the national government with the same objective. Eight of these have been steadily constructed around London since the late 1940s, and over 450,000 people now occupy them.

For example, Hemel Hempstead, in Hertfordshire, is a new town which had a population of 69,500 at the end of 1969, of which 48,300 were migrants, mostly from London. It is twenty-three miles from central London, just beyond the green belt and close to the London-Birmingham motorway. Until December 1969 a total of £45·5 millions had been invested there by the government. A large part of this had been allocated to the building of over 14,000 rented houses even though the town also contained 6,000 privately owned houses.

Industrialists have invested in plants employing nearly 13,100 at Hemel Hempstead and there is a flourishing modern shopping and office centre, as well as a picturesque old high street that has been carefully patched and painted. Also, a new British headquarters for the Kodak Company has been completed and total employment in the town is over 30,000.

It would be futile to pretend that the new towns are beyond criticism. Among the most obvious is the fact that they have failed to aid the poorest and most oppressed Londoners who have tended to stay behind in the inner residential neighbourhoods of the old city. Essentially the residents of the new towns are skilled workers, supervisors, or professionals with the managers and owners living elsewhere. Nevertheless, their balance of homes and jobs, their tree- and park-sprinkled appearance, and their convenient layouts and thriving cultural life make them one of Britain's outstanding recent achievements.

Furthermore, a second generation of new towns, up to seventy miles from London, and twinned with existing towns of about 100,000 people each, is being constructed. Each one is expected to attract or generate enough employment to lure some 75,000 Londoners to it by the 1980s and are located at such places as Peterborough and Northampton. They have already made efforts to attract the less well-off. A new city is also to be built at Milton Keynes, forty minutes up the 100-mile-per-hour electric railway to Birmingham. It is expected to accommodate about 250,000 people by the year 2000. Additional locations for development were announced in a regional development survey for the south-east of England, published by the government in 1970.

Between the metropolis and its satellites is the London green belt. This five-mile-wide strip of countryside is strictly protected from building and keeps the limits of the city virtually within the 1939 boundaries. The area contained inside it measures about thirty-five by about thirty miles and the restrictions on its spread mean that currently about 90,000 people a year move out to find living space. Furthermore, extensions to the green belt have been proposed by all of the home counties although it is accepted that building will continue in these areas.

The new towns are a way of providing for the ordered arrangement of a portion of London's overflow. There remains the need to re-distribute some of the concentration of 1·5 million jobs in central London which are a cause of long commuting journeys, 'sardine-tin' travelling conditions on the tubes and suburban railways, and are a contributory cause of the housing shortage in inner London. Current estimates are that 500,000 routine office jobs could be pro-fitably transferred out of the city although this is a subject of political controversy. Suitable new locations for these jobs are sites like the 'second generation' of new towns. If movement on this scale could be achieved, it would take with it an entire range of lower paying service jobs that now oblige many people to try and make their homes in inner London. The possibility of decentralising 60,000 central government servants is identified in a recent official report.

This is merely a reminder that housing shortages or bad conditions are not solved by building houses alone, but also demand policies for the location of employment and job training extending across the entire sphere of influence of a great city. However, as things stand, it is in inner London, an area of 117 square miles containing 3·2 million people in 1961 at an average density of 27,184 to the square mile, where the main housing problems of the metropolis exist, despite clearance by bombing and an immense amount of reconstruction since the Second World War.

By English standards this old Victorian London is tightly packed with people, although it is notable that the corresponding parts of New York, Manhattan Island and Brooklyn, contained 44,139 persons per square mile in 1960. The central section of Paris is even more jammed with people. But the English process of city con-struction has always been to provide houses with gardens, or at least yards, and not merely flats. Such a low-density tradition is one that has been strongly maintained in the new and expanding towns.

Responsibility for dealing with the inadequacy of housing in inner London is split between the GLC, which is able to offer needy people, near the centre, houses in the outer suburbs, and the London boroughs. Throughout the London megalopolis there are thirty-two of these smaller-scale authorities, plus the ancient City of London, and they have an average population of 250,000. The inner twelve boroughs bear the burden of redevelopment, but in 1969 the outer ones made 1,000 homes available to families from their hard-pressed inner neighbourhoods.

A measure of the capabilities of these boroughs, which are by no means second-rate, can be observed from the efforts of Camden, a council whose limits extend from the central business district to the fashionable heights of Hampstead. In a typical year, Camden' has £13 millions worth of housing construction and improvement contracts running and employs seventy people on architectural and surveying work at its drawing offices and sites. The GLC has a comparable staff of 350. In addition the GLC has 290 professional and technical staff members working on housing maintenance as well as 6,400 bricklayers, carpenters, and construction workers.

The type of home being built by councils varies with local conditions. Over the country as a whole builders, public and private, are currently putting up three houses for every flat. But the vast majority of the flats are being built by local councils and in the big cities. Thus, in the first quarter of 1970, 28,938 flats and only 7,166 houses were built in Greater London, the majority of the flats being constructed by public authorities.

It is partially the need to achieve densities of 100 persons per acre and over as well as architectural fashion that accounts for so many flats being built. However, high towers of flats have recently received criticism from sociologists as being unsuitable for family life. Children living in them are said to become isolated from playmates and to have too few opportunities to go out-of-doors and enjoy nature. On the other hand, many tenants do not have young children and more than half the flats started by councils in the first half of 1967 were in blocks of five floors or less.

The government has recently introduced new cost limits that discourage high building except when it is unavoidable. At the same time, some of the more interesting designs emerging from the offices of local authorities and private architects are for low-level solutions to high density housing. Many of these consist of buildings three to four storeys high with occasional seven-storey buildings representing an upper limit. Such an approach is found superior to the very high density low buildings and costs less than the very tall ones as well as providing greater convenience for the occupants. The architects department of the borough of Southwark is a leader in this field and has shown how houses with gardens can be designed at densities of approximately 100 persons per acre.

The GLC built a delightful 'nest' of little urban cottages with gardens at a similar density at Angrave Street, Shoreditch, a few years ago, but is dubious about building large areas of such low level, high density housing. The architectural firm of Higgins & Ney has used a different approach in a group of houses with a broad outdoor footway at second-floor level (comparable to third floor in the USA) for the borough of Hammersmith. This enables two-storey family houses to be placed on top of flats for the elderly while still giving the houses front doors that open out on to a place where children can play. Another experiment in building at a still higher density (200 persons per acre is permitted in London's West End) is being completed for Westminster City Council at Lillington Street only a thousand yards from Buckingham Palace. This development contains homes of various sizes grouped around grassy courtyards, and is the work of another young firm of architects, Darbourne & Darke. They were awarded the job several years ago in a borough-sponsored competition.

The Royal Institute of British Architects estimates that between 33 and 35 per cent of local authority housing is designed by architects in private practice and that together with the more progressive official architects they are an important source for fresh ideas. On the other hand, official architects are in a better position to promote standard procedures and details from their experience with large building programmes. They are also better placed to utilise the skills of traffic engineers, sociologists, valuation experts and housing managers in the design of houses.

Furthermore, large local authority housing programmes have played an important part in making homes from factories possible. During the 1960s the purchasing power of councils has led to a mush-rooming of towers of flats of ten storeys and more built of large pre-cast slabs of concrete. Already under attack on social grounds, the results of this technical innovation recently received a further setback when a twenty-one-storey block collapsed, like a 'card house', in East London with the loss of five lives. Efforts have accordingly been switched to simplifying the construction of row houses in order to obtain economies in cost and greater speed in this kind of building.

As a result of these initiatives the number of houses and flats built by industrialised methods of all kinds increased in England and Wales from 17,171 in 1964 to 53,150 in 1969, or 38 per cent of all local authority construction. This was the outcome of deliberate government pressure designed to expand the capacity of the building industry and force its modernisation while keeping the demand for building labour fairly static.

The government pressure has not been without its financial cost—but the gain has been dwellings that would otherwise not have been built. In 1965, factory-made dwellings of all kinds (excluding caravans) worked out at £0·18* a square foot more than those built by traditional means. However, by the summer of 1970 this gap had been closed and industrial methods were cheaper by £0·22* per square foot. And, by the same date, factory-made flats were working out £0·75 per square foot cheaper than traditional construction in the higher, and therefore very expensive, blocks. There has also been a spin-off of new managerial techniques into the world of bricks and mortar building.

The current situation can therefore be summed up by saying that the efforts of both architects and promoters of factory-made homes are being concentrated on achieving, as nearly as possible, the old English ideal of the house with a garden, even in inner London. The benefits of such an approach are simple. The cost of lower buildings is less than the average flat built by the London boroughs in 1968 (£4,468), whereas the average two-storey house cost £3,678. There is also a reduced risk of social deprivation.

The calculation of rents is a complicated business, but current practice is to push them up towards what is called 'fair rent' level. This is arrived at by subtracting from market rents the element attributed to scarcity. Rebates are offered to tenants whose incomes are inadequate to pay the increased rents. The extent to which municipal rents have been increased in Greater London is indicated by the rise in the weekly average from 28s 1d in April 1961 to 47s 7d (or £123 per year) in October 1967. This rise is, however, partly explained by inflation and by the addition of more spacious and expensive homes to the stock. It should also be considered against the 1967 average annual income for council households of £1,350. The comparable figure for owner-occupiers with mortgages was £1,840.

Fair rents vary with the age, location, and quality of individual houses. Thus, an inter-war house with three bedrooms at one of the GLC's outer suburban estates (i.e. Becontree) has had a 'fair rent' of £3·50 a week, a post-war house at the same place would bear a rent of £4·25, and a 1962 flat of similar size, in a tall block near the West End

* £0·18 and £0·22 is the new decimal currency.

(Warwick Estate, Paddington), would bear a rent of £6·00 with heating, water and property taxes excluded. Actually, the whole 'Fair Rent' scheme is so much in the public eye that actual rents are difficult to quote because the situation is so fluid.

The problem with all this and with Britain's municipal houses in general, is that they do not sufficiently serve the needs of the poorest people. A simple illustration of this, from the 1966 census, is the predicament of those households with very low incomes—under £500 a year. Such households would mainly constitute retired couples or single persons. With such tiny resources it might be expected that many families would live in council houses where they could be subsidised, though in the past council houses have been built primarily for families with children. However, although this emphasis has been changing, council housing is such a complex subject that measurable changes do not happen fast. Few of this low-income group would be expected to live in privately rented homes where the only benefits available to them are through the Ministry of Social Security but, in fact, the reverse is the case. Only 12 per cent, or 588,000, of the 4·9 million council tenants are in this income group, compared with 22 per cent, or 748,000, of the 3·4 million tenants of private landlords.

This is one reason why extra efforts are being made to change the country's housing policies. A private Act of Parliament has already been passed to enable the city of Birmingham to pay subsidies to poor families in privately rented accommodation, and London is studying the idea. Also, one of the objects in raising municipal rents to higher levels is the expectation that more prosperous tenants will find it cheaper to move out and pay for a mortgage. In some places, council houses are even being sold—over 8,590 in 1969—although not without a political storm. Low interest mortgages have also been introduced to extend housing purchases to a wider circle of householders.

Meanwhile a new Housing Bill was passed in 1969 that will provide increased grants and loans for improving and repairing old homes as well as for planting trees, creating playgrounds and building garages amongst them. In areas where such improvements are carried out, the rent of privately rented accommodation is being freed from rent control. Controls of one sort or another have been in existence since the 1914–18 war, with disastrous effects on standards of repair and on investment in the modernisation of older property.

2

However, there is now the prospect of a free market in housing in Britain, within the next ten to fifteen years.

These same house improvement powers are also leading to local authorities buying and modernising older homes. From the tenant's point of view this is often welcome because improvement costs less than rebuilding with the result that rents are lower. From the community's point of view it is an advantage to keep neighbourhoods going which does not happen when the bulldozers move in; and it is also desirable to keep the country's stock of old houses in good condition. Furthermore, modernisation is not so much a substitute for new building as a supplement.

But, although changes are near, this does not mean that past efforts have been misapplied. Huge numbers of families have been accommodated in well-built, attractively designed homes that they could not otherwise have afforded.

Furthermore, the most notable failure of Britain's housing policy, inability to get more subsidised houses into the hands of the really poor, has had one most desirable side effect. Council houses are not thought of as places primarily for 'down and outs'. Their occupants tend to think of themselves as respectable people living in respectable homes and while owner-occupiers may consider themselves superior they do not look down upon council tenants.

In fact, the social standing of council estates varies. Where estates are in poor quarters or near large industrial parks, employing many semi-skilled people, they reflect such facts. Yet as the 1966 census showed, 14 per cent of the households in municipal homes earned £2,100 a year or more, a respectable middle-class income.

The architecture and landscape design of the best council homes is as good as any in the country. A measure of this is the way official architects regularly win awards, although, in some cases, for types of housing that private builders do not attempt.

The high quality of municipal housing can have unexpected results. In Sheffield, a city with a reputation for good municipal housing design, a social survey revealed that some owner-occupiers thought that neighbouring council tenants lived in homes superior to their own. An indication of what architects working for councils should aim at recently came to the attention of the designer of an attractive series of pink brick houses in a Sussex village. The tenants were particularly pleased with them because they resembled houses built for sale.

The main characteristics of popular council houses and flats are quite simple. They are sited within convenient distance of shops and public transport; there are opportunities for women to go out to work nearby; the homes are quite close to their garages and have kitchens large enough to eat in; existing trees around them are carefully preserved and new ones planted; they are built of warm and attractive materials suited to the neighbourhood; they are off main roads and served by footpaths that underpass the roads on the way to schools and shops; and they are provided with communal sand-pits and wading pools for the children. In fact, the recipe is the same as it is for homes for sale.

Another aspect of housing that is under re-evaluation is the mixing up of different types of people. For better or worse, social diversity is never easy to achieve in towns. Builders tend to build for different income groups in different places, and generations also tend to divide up. No doubt this is to some extent what people want and local authorities have tended to contribute to this parcelling up of groups because they have built predominantly for families. Thus, over 80 per cent of the annual output of council houses have regularly had two or three bedrooms.

In places like London where there is an above average concentration of one- and two-person households, this had led to hardship which is only now being recognised. An illustration of the new thinking is a block of small flats being built by the Ministry of Housing research and development group in Leicester. And in Harlow, a new town in Essex, over 1,000 small homes have been built to enable London's families moving out to take their retired parents with them without the need to live on top of one another.

In summary, it is important to stress the fact that Londoners' houses are only one part of a triangle of themes—jobs, homes and transport—all of which play a dominant part in shaping the quality of urban life. At present, the scene in Britain is changing. Efforts are being made, though with strong opposition, to steer the existing stock of public authority homes in the direction of the lower-income families. At the same time, attempts are being made to see that houses for middle- and lower-income families are near to one another and do not become isolated into different camps. More and more effort is being spent on the renewing of old neighbourhoods by street improvements and the selective clearing and rebuilding of old houses, or out of place workshops, instead of bulldozing whole districts. The possibility of using urban motorways, not just as speedy through-ways but as elements in corridors of renewal, designed by architects as well as engineers, is being discussed. Only by continuously re-assessing past achievements and testing new ideas in this way, is there any hope of doing something about the families who still have no proper homes or who are still without modern kitchens, bathrooms and heating.

Chapter 3   Public Housing in France
The HLM

MAURICE LANGLET

Low- and moderate-income housing (*Habitations à Loyer Modéré*, or HLM) occupies an essential place in French housing policy in the 1970s. It permits large groups of people with moderate incomes to live in safe, sanitary and sound modern housing.

Providing adequate housing for people of modest means is among the primary problems of our age. The first housing law in France, passed in 1894, was designed to stimulate the creation of private building companies. In 1906, some public participation in the building was enlisted but was largely restricted to the lowest-income families. At the same time municipalities were encouraged to help building companies by giving them financial aid or land.

In 1908, legislation empowered Building Mortgage Societies to help workers acquire their own homes. In 1912, a law created public companies which were to be initiated and managed by local authorities (HBM*). However, it was not until the end of the First World War that there were any significant changes. At that time the government started building low-cost housing in earnest, as opposed to the token efforts made earlier when the main thrust was left to subsidised private builders. The primary reason for the increased government activity in 1919 was the introduction of a rent control system which aimed at protecting families by keeping down rents and prices. As a result, little money was invested in modernising homes and even less in new building. After the gap between demand and supply widened sharply, the government stepped in.

From 1919 to 1939 the state provided subsidies to offset the difference between the current interest rate on loans and the interest rate necessary to bring rents down to a manageable level for low-income families. During this period more government aid was also extended to those wishing to own homes (*Accession à la Propriété*). By 1939, HBM had built 320,000 units; about 170,000 for rent and

* *Habitations à Bon Marché*

37

about 150,000 (45 per cent) for ownership. An expanded programme in 1946 emphasised an increase of rental apartments for low- and moderate-income families.

The change of the term HBM (low-income housing) to HLM (moderate-income housing) took place in 1950 because the already limited stock of housing became even more inadequate as the rate of demand accelerated. This demand was created by an increased birth rate, an increased migration to the cities, war damage, increased foreign immigration, an increase in inadequate housing, and urban renewal programmes. From 1946 to 1953, 70,000 units (about 10,000 per year) were constructed in France for HLM; one-seventh of the 500,000 built during the eight years immediately following the war. This slow beginning—HLM units totalled only 390,000 in 1953—resulted from the lack of financial resources and the fact that the building industry had to be completely reorganised and redeveloped. By 1970, however, 1,550,000 rental units had been built by HLM; 665,000 for sale. Since 1970 an average of more than 200,000 units per year has been constructed. In terms of rental as opposed to ownership units, there was about a $2\frac{1}{2}$ to 1 ratio in housing production during the period, reflecting the general governmental decision that there should be more emphasis on rental units, as a result of the post-war needs.

As the trend moved towards producing an increased proportion of rental units, there also developed an increase in the ratio between public-versus-private units. In the 1956–63 period, 15 per cent of the units built were of public construction. By 1970, public housing in France represented 35 per cent of all housing constructed, two million units (15 per cent) out of the fifteen million housing stock. At the current rate of building, this percentage may again move upwards. The administrators are constantly attempting to supply more housing and, today, the amount of housing built is solely dependent upon the amount of monies annually put at the disposal of the local HLM. The functions of the HLM public companies and societies are to develop the programme, acquire the property, design the buildings and construct and manage the housing.

In France, the public housing agencies take into account physical and aesthetic needs of the population as much as possible, limited by financial and technical restrictions. Increasingly, the stark, barrack-type housing, characteristic of post-Second World War housing, is being eliminated. More homes have been developed employing the use of as much green space as density and land costs permit. As an indispensable part of social progress HLM accepts the responsibility of providing comfortable, safe housing and to meet current needs.

With the increased demand for homes, and because the price of standard, comfortable housing has increased more than salary scales, an increasing number of people find it impossible to buy or rent in the private market and turn to HLM. As a result, HLM has been obliged to diversify its housing programmes, appealing to a broader level of families, without relaxing its emphasis upon the needs of families in the lowest income groups. With the assistance of the central government, the local HLM organisations have developed: (a) dwelling units with social services aimed at the needs of families with low and moderate income; (b) dwelling units for young married white-collar workers; (c) special programmes for the aged, young blue-collar workers, and students; and finally, (d) programmes of urban rehabilitation such as razing of slums and urban renewal of below standard and unsanitary housing.

The responsibility for building in HLM has been distributed in a variety of ways between 1,300 HLM agencies; among which are 307 public offices for low-cost housing, 212 HLM mortgage companies and 244 HLM housing co-operatives. The HLM agencies are public and quasi-public establishments, about 300 of which were created and are operated by the municipalities or local 'departments' (the French equivalent of states or provinces). The local authorities are responsible for planning and constructing rental dwellings for families of low and moderate means, but they can also plan and carry out urban renewal programmes. Legislation in July 1971 enlarged the field of activity of the public HLM offices and transformed them into public establishments of a commercial and industrial character in order to relieve them of administrative matters and help make them more efficient. These offices not only construct housing for rent and ownership but also act as planners for the local housing programme.

Another 300 of the HLM offices are quasi-public HLM limited companies, having their origin in 1908 under the HBM programme. These companies help with construction loans. Though authorised by the government, they were created by private initiative and operated by community organisations, such as public savings banks, organisations administering the family allowance programmes, or professional groups interested in housing their local personnel.

These organisations primarily build rental housing, under the same conditions as the local public HLM offices.

HLM mortgage companies were begun in 1908 and are another type of quasi-public stock company authorised by the Ministry of Housing. Their object is to afford financial help to people of modest means who wish to own either a single-family detached home or a house in a subdivision of single-family homes constructed by a building company associated with an HLM mortgage company.

In addition to being eligible for government loans, such building companies can secure mortgages from the French National Mortgage Bank (*Crédit Foncier de France*) plus a forfeiture rent subsidy. A recent law enlarged the field of activity of these HLM mortgage companies and they are now able to initiate building programmes directly, under certain restrictions.

There are, in addition, co-operative societies of the HLM made possible by the law of April 1906 which function under the Ministry of Housing. These societies construct buildings both for co-operative rentals and through the co-operative make them available for home ownership. The co-operative society puts at the disposal of its members a rental unit with the option or guarantee of ultimately turning it into ownership. The two parties, society and individual, contract together in ownership. After paying the cost of the dwelling (twenty-five year maximum) the occupant becomes the owner.

A second method of operation is a rental programme guaranteeing the tenant the right to live permanently in a dwelling with no fear of being evicted because of family or income changes. The tenant makes a deposit of at least 10 per cent of the original costs of the occupied housing and subscribes to the society for a sum equal to the loan contract with the society.

In return for financial assistance to the HLM companies, the state has permanent and direct supervisory powers over these organisations exercised through the Ministry of Community Facilities and Housing, as well as the Ministry of Economic Affairs and Finance. The ministries exercise these controls over technical, accounting, administrative and financial matters. The prefecture is responsible for seeing that the ministries' requirements are carried out.

The nature of the HLM rental dwellings, according to the current regulations, is dictated by construction demands. All dwellings are administered by the local public offices of HLM. The various categories are as follows:

PSR (*Programme social de relogement*) is a programme of providing relocation housing. Many of the people it houses are immigrants—ejected from slum areas or deteriorated buildings condemned to be demolished.

PLR (*Programme de loyer réduit*) is a low-income housing programme. The units are comfortable and meet more than the minimum standards. HLM has no difficulty in filling vacancies. The rents of PLR flats are very low since the HLM local offices receive low rate construction loans from the government at 1 per cent over forty-five years. The flats contain few amenities, but they do have central heating, washrooms and toilets, and kitchens. A large number (12,000) of these dwellings were built in 1970, but their number will decrease in the coming years, largely because of the high financial cost they represented in the national budget and also because the government believes that such dwellings create social segregation. A greater number of the HLM/O type will be constructed instead. A dwelling allowance will compensate for the higher rent.

HLM/O (*Habitations à loyer modéré-ordinaire*) These units, representing the bulk of the HLM programme in the last few years, are constructed in conformity with all standards and norms. They assure comfort, safety, and adequate space. They satisfy all contemporary needs and are equivalent to current building in the private sector.

ILN (*Immeuble à loyer normal*) and *ILM* (*Immeuble à loyer moyen*) These buildings are constructed by HLM for people with incomes slightly higher than the eligibility level of HLM but who still cannot afford private housing. With moderate rental, the quality of these units is somewhat more luxurious, the facilities a little better. However, little financing is available for these units and their number is not large.

Lodgings-Foyers-Efficiency Apartments are provided for older people, young migrant workers, and single people. They are a type of hotel with four- or five-room bedroom units grouped around a kitchen, a living/dining-room, and other related service rooms. They are operated by private non-profit societies. In some instances, they are one-room efficiency apartments.

University Residences are constructed in conjunction with the Ministry of Education and are for students.

2*

HLM Ownership Programmes (*Accession à la Propriété*) in which the home ownership approach to housing is an important facet of the total programme. In 1970 it represented about one out of four of the total HLM housing stock. Units consist of individual homes, homes in subdivisions, or apartments in a large complex. The maximum floor area is about 10 per cent higher than that of HLM flats. The general construction norms are the same as for the other HLM programmes. In applying for home ownership, the applicant's space, number of rooms, and total allowable expense will be more limited than in a building that has not received government support. Also, the income rules are more restricted. There is a marked tendency, particularly outside the big cities to use this ownership or co-operative scheme to own homes or at least have the right of sole occupation.

The extremely high cost of land in the large cities makes it difficult to carry on building operations in the inner city, or even on the perimeter of such areas, and still keep within the limits of the cost regulations established for HLM by the government. To avoid the high cost problem, group dwellings have been built in outlying areas, but this may constitute a form of segregation for low- and moderate-income families which is socially unjust and inadvisable. While the cleavage is not as great as in many countries, it is not considered salutary and efforts are made to avoid such placements. However, since the income level of HLM eligibles in many instances approaches the median income level, the threat of segregation does not loom too large.

The acquisition of acceptable land is a delicate problem for local authorities. The need for social control of land is felt most acutely in the industrial areas and is a direct function of demographic shifts in these industrial regions, where the cost of land suitable for building is very high. Some measures have been taken to halt the increase in land prices during the last twenty years. Unfortunately, these have proved to be completely ineffective and the situation has tended to deteriorate with frightening speed. Land prices around urban areas double every eight to ten years.

Providing for 'Areas of Planned Improvement' (*Zones d'Aménagement Concert*, or ZAC) located in rural areas has not really stopped the increase in prices. In most cases, the base price of the land for agricultural use is not taken into account and the majority of this rural acreage is sold as building land, at five to ten times the price of agricultural land.

In addition, by way of the ZAC concept, present government policy has shifted from a regulated urbanisation to a contractual one. This has enabled the public sector to reduce financial aid to housing developments and place much of the financial burden on the builders, whether public or private.

In some ZACs in particular, the HLM organisation has to bear the cost of land improvement and even sometimes to participate in the financing of community services such as schools, firehouses, etc. From now on it seems that the government will limit its intervention to large urban operations of the 'New Town' type through the use of its 'Economic and Social Development Fund'.

In addition, some 'Deferred Development Areas' (*Zones d'Aménagement Différé*, or ZAD) have been created in order to stem the price increases. In fact, the prime advantage of these ZADs resides in the exercise of a pre-emptive right in order to benefit the public. Price stability was never achieved because the real estate assessors, guardians of private property in the pure tradition of French law, have appraised land values on the basis of market value. This is also true of appraisals made by the control committees which oversee real estate transactions.

Along with lower land costs, an important control of building costs is control of technical building standards. Since 1955, French legislative manuals have codified the rules of all dwelling construction. Construction was expected to conform to rules promulgated by the National Construction Code set forth in 'Technical Manual of Rules and Minimal Functional Standards'. However, to expedite construction, many of the specific restrictions of the manual have been set aside. Nevertheless, builders must adhere to the general plans and rules of urbanisation, as well as to the general rules on construction relative to fire hazards, health hazards and telecommunications. Building controls are, in the main, utilised to improve rather than inhibit social planning.

After the modification of the 'Technical Manual of Rules and Minimal Functional Standards', the National Federation of HLM Organisations published 'General Technical Rules' recommending a minimum level of amenities and equipment and the particular rules that apply to the multi-unit dwellings of HLM. When the government contributes substantially to the financing of construction, or the management of the project, it maintains the right to require conformity with the particular regulations designated under 'HLM Rules'. The rules are principally concerned with dimensional characteristics and maximum net costs of the housing and these standards differ according to the type of financing and the type of housing. The most recent manuals show significant improvements in housing standards, particularly in the amount of living space. For example, in a five-room flat for two adults and two children, the minimum living area is eighty square metres; a fairly good size compared with standards in other countries of Europe. A three-room flat must have between fifty-five and sixty-three square metres as well as a kitchen, laundry room, inside WC, central heating, rubbish chute and supply of hot water.

One of the other factors in reducing building costs is prefabrication or industrialisation of building. Indispensable to prefabrication is the building of housing complexes. Such complexes were initiated to assure construction of good quality at maximum efficiency and a fair price. The complex is a group of building projects characterised by size and variety of site, opportunity for individual and community ownership and special financing. The common denominator from area to area is the procedure of construction. Even where building is traditional, as in the case of individual homes, processes of construction have to be industrialised because the precision of jobs and procedural approach on the site requires it. The general policy behind the building of these complexes is to afford a reduction in construction cost along with the maintenance of quality.

Such complexes are under continuous study to evaluate the quality of prefabricated housing in accordance with methods developed by the French Centre for Technical and Scientific Building (CSTB). In certain geographic areas, with the agreement of the municipality, building groups from the centre study the projects to be completed on sites of their choice. When the site is acquired and prepared for building, and a 'ready to build' licence has been obtained from the ministry, the groups contact private builders and HLM agencies likely to be interested in building the project.

Under the pre-1970 regulations relating to loans for social housing, definite price ceilings were applied to 'construction costs only' in order to keep prices down. However, other costs and prices were included in the total cost of production and were less controlled. Nevertheless, a total maximum cost could not be exceeded. After

November 1970 two cost ceilings were established: one for construction costs and the other for land costs, improvements and surveying.

Another significant change was made in March 1970 when price ceilings on construction cost were reduced from 900F per square metre to 700F in the provinces and from 1,200F to 900F in the Paris region. On the other hand, initial government financing covers 90–95 per cent of construction costs. This virtually complete government financing makes it somewhat easier for the citizen in the low- and moderate-income groups to obtain housing, while the stringent cost ceiling regulations insure that new housing will be restricted to these families.

Moreover, while construction cost ceilings were formerly applied on a square metre basis, the 1970 regulations have fixed ceiling prices according to type of dwelling (whether one bedroom, two bedrooms, or five bedrooms) but do not vary the cost according to square metres involved. The distinctions may not seem great but it is again intended to give more flexibility to builders. However, the new regulations of 1970 apply to less than half the buildings—those constructed for home ownership.

Marked differences exist between construction costs of the smallest unit and the largest, and in Paris compared with the provinces. For the smallest efficiency unit the maximum is 15,000F for an owned apartment and 16,200F for an individual home with maximum loan possibility of 13,500F for an average flat of two bedrooms for two adults and two children. The maximum total cost for an apartment is 47,000F and for an individual home 51,000F, with a maximum mortgage value of 42,500F for the apartment and 42,500F for the home. (See Table 1 on owned homes on following page.)

In translating construction costs plus land costs into rents or monthly payments in the form of debt service, the crucial question is the type and amount of loans available. Two decrees of 1966 created the HLM loan fund (*Caisse de Prêt HLM*). This fund has been supplied with funds from the government, about 50 per cent from its authorised loans and the remainder from borrowings from *Caisse de Dépots et Consignations*. The funds are loaned to local HLM organisations on terms and rates fixed by national regulations.

For HLM rental units the interest rates and terms are 2·95 per cent for forty years for the HLM/O units and 1 per cent for forty-five

TABLE 1 Construction Cost Limits, by Living Area, Mortgage Loan Limits and Income Limits by Family Composition. Applicable from January, 1970 for Units Under Programme of Home Ownership HLM

			Characteristics of units and loans					Maximum Monthly Income of Beneficiary		
Type of dwelling	Living area in square metres		Multiple unit housing subdivisions		Maximum cost price individual homes		Maximum loan granted to HLM	Family Composition	One wage earner	Several wage earners
	Minimum	Maximum	Price all expenses included	Construction cost alone	Price of expenses included	Construction cost alone				
A	B	C	D	E (=70% D)	F (=108% D)	G (=70% F)	H	I	J	K
			F.	F.	F.	F.	F.		F.	F.
I	14	22	15,000	10,500	16,200	11,340	13,500	One person	900	—
I	25	36	24,750	17,325	26,730	18,711	22,275	Two persons	1,050	1,250
II	42	55	37,500	26,250	40,500	28,350	33,750	Three persons or young family with less than 5 years of marriage		
III	55	69	47,250	33,075	51,030	35,721	42,525	Four persons	1,250	1,550
IV	66	85	57,750	40,425	62,370	43,659	51,975	Five persons	1,450	1,800
V	80	102	69,750	48,825	75,330	52,731	62,775	Six persons	1,700	2,100
VI	90	121	82,500	57,750	89,100	62,370	74,250	More than Six persons	1,950	2,450
VII	110	137	93,750	65,625	101,250	70,875	84,375		+250	+350

years for PLR and PSR. Moreover, 95 per cent of the total net cost can be financed in the case of HLM/O and PSR and PLR. The remaining 5 per cent can be obtained in any of several ways: from the Fund for Family Allowance, from the local community, from private resources or from the contributions of the employers of more than ten employees who are assessed at 1 per cent of their payroll for housing expenditures. This 1 per cent is an investment of the firms in the building of homes and performs an important public service while providing help for their own employees who require it. Investments must be made for a minimum period of twenty years and can only be used in new building or in 'repair' loans granted by real estate 'credit' companies.

For those families interested in buying homes through HLM, building organisations grant loans of between 80-90 per cent of the total cost. Also in these loans a 2·5 per cent subsidy is available for the first five years and a 1 per cent subsidy for the second five years; considerably reducing the 5 per cent for the first ten years of the loan.

Efficiency dwellings, for aged persons or single individuals, are also financed by up to 85-90 per cent of the total cost.

In order to bring the cost of these HLM dwellings within reach of people of low and moderate means, a number of subsidies are available over and above the low interest rates. Families having more than one child receive a housing subsidy from the Fund for Family Allowances. Some 'Departments' (Counties) may give special subsidies to very low income families. Certain advantages are also obtained by employees in organisations employing more than ten employees. Young families without children may apply for certain concessions during their first two years of marriage. Additional housing subsidies are granted to families paying up to 250F per month rent. Also, in fixing eligibility the income of a married woman is not counted during the first five years of her marriage and only 50 per cent of the income of working children is considered. Finally, for persons seeking to own their own home, certain subsidies or advantages are available from local savings banks or banks primarily engaged in making building loans.

Rental level is determined on the basis of a classification of all dwellings, according to size and income level, in relation to the maximum level and minimum rent needed to operate each unit. Rents are adjusted by multiplying adjusted living area by the price per square metre and then using the minimum price necessary to operate the units without a deficit, along with a maximum price based on the market value of the unit; the aim is to have rents at a level to meet all expenses and yet be as fair as possible. On an average, HLM rents are 30–35 per cent less than rents of unsubsidised flats with the same amenities and living space and in the same locality.

The rental of each project is dependent on the quality, size and condition of the project, as well as the operating conditions. The rent includes a provision for reserve, for replacement, for maintenance and for repair. However, many small maintenance or up-keep costs are directly traceable to tenant neglect. The HLM agencies try to explain to the tenants that derelictions on their part, in defacing walls, stair-halls or lawns, have to be handled by the local managers and are ultimately chargeable back to the tenants in the form of rent increases. Where possible such charges are made to the individual tenants or shared on a pro rata basis depending on the circumstances.

A recent practice is to charge a surcharge rent for tenants whose incomes have moved far above the eligibility line for admission, rather than ask them to move. These charges are imposed only when the income has risen more than 15 per cent over the income level (in the case of PSR and PLR) and more than 20 per cent in the case of HLM/O and ILM units. In general only about 8 per cent of families have been affected in the provinces and 20 per cent in the Paris region.

Rentals in France do not regularly include services charged separately to the tenants through an assessment by management. On the one hand, while large repairs are the responsibility of managements of HLM, such charges as maintenance of public and open spaces, gas, electricity, hot water, heating of public space, and cleaning of chimneys are passed back to the tenant.

Occupancy of a dwelling under HLM is subject to a number of conditions. For admission to HLM/O in France generally (excluding Paris), the income for a four-person family cannot exceed 2,050F per month with one wage earner or 2,500F per month with several wage earners. For the Paris region, it is about 10 per cent higher. Income limits vary according to the size of the family. For ILM dwellings the income limits are somewhat higher and for PSR and PLR they are somewhat lower. (See Table 2.)

The second condition of occupancy relates to living conditions and occupation of the individual family. Essentially the conditions

TABLE 2 *Rental Apartments. Table of Ceiling Monthly Income Allowable for Admission Compared With Wages Schedule, January 1970*

Categories of HLM housing	Geographical zones	One person	Two persons		Recent married with less than 5 yrs of marriage and 4 persons		Four persons		Five persons		Six persons	
			One wage earner	Several wage earners	One wage earner	Several wage earners	One wage earner	Several wage earners	One wage earner	Several wage earners	One wage earner	Several wage earners
		F	F	F	F	F	F	F	F	F	F	F
HLM/O	All areas except Paris	1,250	1,500	1,750	1,750	2,200	2,050	2,500	2,400	2,950	2,750	3,450
	Paris	1,400	1,700	1,950	1,950	2,450	2,250	2,800	2,650	3,300	3,000	3,750
PLR PSR, etc.	All areas except Paris	1,000	1,150	1,350	1,350	1,700	1,550	1,900	1,850	2,250	2,100	2,600
	Paris	1,050	1,250	2,500	2,500	1,900	1,700	2,100	2,050	2,500	2,300	2,850
ILM	All areas except Paris	1,900	2,250	2,650	2,650	3,300	3,100	3,750	3,550	4,400	4,100	5,150
	Paris	2,100	2,500	2,950	2,950	3,700	3,350	4,200	4,000	4,950	4,550	5,650

(I) If the family has more than 6 people the amount allowable is increased on a per capita basis as follows:

for HLM/O—350F for one wage earner, 500F where there are several wage earners

for PLR/PSR etc.—300F for one wage earner, 350F for several wage earners

for ILM—600F for one wage earner, 800F more than one wage earner

Note: Essentially this table is to be used as an indicator, not the final word particularly when there are bonuses received, or unearned income.

governing eligibility, while developed by the locality, are established nationally. Factors include degree of overcrowding, degree of substandardness, conditions of occupation such as whether the tenant's employer has contributed to the project, or any other agreements made by the HLM organisation regarding tenancy at the time of construction. Likewise, conditions considered before deciding eligibility for admission include living in a hotel or furnished lodging inadequate to family needs, in a unit destined for demolition, in a unit with less than four square metres per person, a unit where the lease is up and non-renewable, where an eviction notice is pending for reasons other than non-payment of rent or undesirability, or where the unit is unfit for habitation.

Tenants are chosen by the HLM agencies or by a commission composed of local representatives of HLM, the local community and the prefect's office (which in France is a representative of the national government in the *département*). In Paris, for example, 70 per cent of the tenants are admitted in accordance with an application list of HLM but 30 per cent are chosen from a priority list established by the prefect. The increase in population both in Paris proper and in the Paris region in the last years, plus the high cost of land, makes the problems particularly difficult for low- and moderate-income families and the problems of distributive justice even keener.

About 27 per cent of all the HLM units are owner-occupied and during the last three years about 20 per cent of all units constructed were intended for ownership.

The maximum cost of construction for home ownership under HLM is outlined in Table 1. Under the 1970 law, applicable to 20,000 of the 35,000 units put into service that year, the maximum cost for an individual home for a family of four is 57,750F. At least 70 per cent of the expenses must be spent on construction cost alone. The top loan to be allowed is 51,975F. Under these conditions, it is difficult to build for home ownership in the Paris region.

Although a number of different subsidies are available for families who wish to purchase, the percentage of purchasers in the last few years has been somewhat less than in the past. Looking at it in another perspective, since the number of people in the ownership programme hovered around 30,000 for the last several years and the number in the rental programme increased more sharply, more emphasis has been placed on this programme.

Nevertheless, to aid the movement towards ownership, co-operative societies grant financial aid for the acquisition, improvement, or enlargement of older properties. When it is one of these and the buyer either wishes to improve it, enlarge it, or restore it to its original condition, in the case of homes built before 1947, different subsidies are available. Extensive use is made of these rehabilitation loans although the total amounts are considerably less than for new units. In the renovation of buildings, the total amount available for loans for enlarging or modernising any single building cannot exceed 7,800F. Loans for acquisition plus rehabilitation cannot exceed 23,500F. In order to assure that these loans are used specifically for rehabilitation rather than merely for purchase of older homes, it is provided that at least 40 per cent of the loan must be used for the actual construction cost of putting the home into shape. It is also provided that the loan can only be used for a home in which the applicant lives or wishes to live and is not available for speculative or business purposes.

Conclusions

In spite of the enterprising efforts in France over the past twenty-five years, housing still poses many questions, among which are the volume of housing to be provided and the persons to whom the programme should be directed.

A recent study by the administration points up that among the households able to aspire to an HLM dwelling within the next few years, about 30 per cent have an annual income of less than 10,000F. Since the net cost of the two-bedroom unit, the most commonly needed unit for the family, is around 50,000F and, under HLM, the amount of annual rent is 3,000F, many families with incomes of 5,000 to 10,000F per year cannot afford such housing. This means that in the years to come renewed effort has to be made by the HLM and the government to reduce the cost of housing or to provide additional subsidies in order to meet the housing needs of the lowest segment of the population.

Chapter 4 Public Housing in Israel

ISRAEL SHAHAM

Israel's economic and social development since the country gained its independence in 1948 is marked by three special characteristics:

Mass Immigration where the individual immigrant is faced with the necessity of adapting himself to the conditions prevailing in his new country.

Development of Resources includes physical, economic and social development at a spiralling pace: development of water and power resources; discovery and exploitation of mineral resources; the growth of various branches of the economy; the expansion of housing, education and health services.

Increase of Population extends the expansion of populated areas by the establishment of new villages and towns in unpopulated, poorly populated and abandoned localities.

Immigration, combined with the other realities of Israel, is far more than a simple demographic or economic factor. Under the Law of Return, the first basic law passed in Israel after independence, every Jew is free to emigrate to Israel, to return to the land of his forefathers. The most consistently pursued policy in Israel is that all immigrants should be provided with good shelter. The following figures indicate the growth of the new nation, whose population increased by 318 per cent within twenty years, and point up the problem Israel faces in its housing needs.

Israel's Jewish Population and the Source of its Increase 1948–70

Population	Natural Increase	Immigration	Total Increase	Total Jewish Population
May 1948	1948–70			December 1970
649,600	756,700	1,155,100	1,911,800	2,561,400

These figures do not begin to hint at the significance of the problems of integrating people coming into a new land from over seventy different countries; each group bringing with it separate customs, ways of life, levels of education, conditioned reflexes and reactions. To forge these heterogeneous groups or tribes into one modern nation, into one way of life, is the greatest challenge of Israeli society.

Immigrants To Israel Classified According to Continents of Origin 1948–67 in per cent.

Continent	%
Europe	42·6
Africa	29·6
Asia	24·2
America & Oceania	3·6
	100·0

Expansion of populated areas is closely connected with immigration. The great majority of the Jewish population, prior to independence (1948), was concentrated, with the exception of Jerusalem, in the narrow coastal strip, due to the restrictions to which Jewish population in Palestine was subjected during the period of the British Mandate which preceded Israel's statehood.

The question of population dispersal is still a central consideration of Israel's national policy. In order to achieve a more balanced development, to avoid an overcrowding of the coastal region and populate the undeveloped zones, it was necessary to adopt a determined and consistent policy of dispersal with respect to large-scale state support of every project, both rural and urban, in the preferred areas.

The history of immigrant housing is actually the history of public housing in Israel. It began in 1948 with immigrant camps where the individual was supplied with food from a central kitchen and provided with health and educational services for his children and social services for him and his family. He had little contact with the world outside the camp. Israeli society was really represented by the camp administration, pursuing public interest frequently opposed to the interest of the individual immigrant. Actually the immigrant camp was outside both the Israeli society and its economy and as soon as possible the camps had to be evacuated and their populations woven into this outside society and economy.

The economy came first but even with modest initial development schemes, it was able to provide jobs for a major part of the new-comers. However, some of the camp dwellers were remnants of the Nazi holocaust, while others were immigrants from some of the most backward countries. Some of them had had their normal economic and social activities terminated in 1939—ten years before—and others had never had a decent chance in all their lives. Evacuation of the camps was therefore crucial. The lesson learned will never be forgotten: the camp experiment would not be repeated again.

The basic idea behind the evacuation was that the immigrant should start working and should start being responsible for both his own fate and that of his family. Evacuation also meant providing additional shelter but there was none to be found as every available apartment and room was already occupied. As a result, shanty towns sprang up. Thousands of twenty-four square metres of bar-racks, huts, tents were erected wherever employment was available, sometimes in the outskirts of towns, sometimes in the heart of the desert.

There was a big difference between those shanty towns and their parallel outside Israel. The *maabaroth*, as they became known, were the focus of public concern. Each *maabara* was provided with public institutions—schools, kindergartens, synagogues, clubs, labour exchanges, nurseries, and medical-care centres. Almost immediately, construction of permanent housing units was started, on the spot. None the less, it took about eighteen years until the last hut concentration disappeared.

The tent and hut suburbs, large and small, disappeared and formed the nucleus of new towns in Israel. All towns, either founded or sizeably increased before 1956, stem from the camps. Most of the camp population were immigrants who were directed there. Some of the immigrants were channelled in the same way to found new villages. New Israel was first and foremost the creation of new immigrants, who were assisted by hundreds of volunteers—social workers, teachers, physicians and nurses, specialists of every kind in crafts, agriculture, industry, and public administration—the pioneers of settlement in the north and south of Israel.

Number of Families in Temporary Housing by Type of Housing 1950-1969.

	1950	1953	1955	1959	1962	1969
Total	70,000	58,200	30,600	19,600	6,000	500
Immigrant camps	48,000	3,200	—	—	—	—
Tents and tin huts	10,000	30,600	6,650	2,900	—	—
Other huts	6,000	18,400	17,650	13,400	3,750	500
British Army huts	6,000	6,000	5,400	3,000	2,250	—
Various structures	—	—	900	300	—	—

During the period when the building of new towns was begun, agriculture was the chief source of livelihood. However, it was soon realised that the new towns had to be based on a much broader economic foundation, i.e. with the development of industry and utilisation of all available potential. The planning of these new towns, therefore, not only considered the architectural and physical aspects of the community but also their economic and social aspects. The programme plan emphasised the following:

(1) Physical and architectural planning regulated the construction and the growth of the town, within the framework of overall development.

(2) Economic planning pointed up the sources of employment and insured an equilibrium between industry, agriculture and services.

(3) Social and community planning worked at establishing a social composition of the population making integration of groups from different countries of origin possible, keeping in mind the welfare of the native or veteran inhabitant of the country on the one hand and the immigrants on the other.

(4) Planning of public services, education, health, entertainment

and supplies were all given special attention. Thirty new towns were built as a result of this programmed planning.

This accomplishment in itself is noteworthy but the Government is by no means satisfied.

Economic targets established for a new community were not always achieved. Perhaps these expectations were too ambitious, but unachieved economic goals also meant a continuation of marginal employment instead of the planned and promised steady, well-paid jobs in industry and services.

The same problem existed in the development of public services. A small, under-developed community has little hope of attracting professional teachers, physicians, nurses and skilled administrators. Therefore, there is little hope for a good education or for developing good health services. In the short run, vacancies may be filled by volunteers or, as was the case, by young female soldiers sent to remote communities to work there during their army service. But the vicious circle is not broken. Without local leadership and an active citizen body, there is little hope for real development in economic and social terms. A new town, like any other public or private enterprise, has to be administered. The administration, at the initial stage, had to be mobilised from outside. 'The right men', from various political caucuses, had done good work. They knew their jobs. They were imbued with a feeling of an idealistic mission. However, most of them failed. With few exceptions they were outsiders of a different mentality, commissioned from above. There was little success in establishing mutual confidence. Even the most gifted town and community builders had to give way to local leadership who were sometimes less competent and not always free from personal or factional ambitions. This 'revolution' was a general problem and virtually no town escaped this cycle of asserted local leadership.

Nor were such 'revolutions' understood. Some regarded them as 'lack of gratitude', others as a kind of dangerous calamity. But the national leadership was quick to accept the new reality and to make the best of it. Developing local leadership in schooling and instruction, by government agencies, trade unions, political parties, proved to be the proper solution. Today, most of the town mayors, trade union leaders, political bosses, and members of Parliament are local products. Several years ago, this would have been inconceivable.

Several new towns have developed autonomously. They have been less dependent on the public 'purse' and are attracting more and more private enterprise. This does, however, cause some difficulty in coping with the sudden increase in population, but public services offered to the population are better and diversified. Beersheba, the capital of the Negev, the southern province, for example, already has a full-scale university and branches of many learned societies.

Apart from the actual construction of new towns is the complementary challenge of integrating heterogeneous groups, of different social backgrounds, different habits, belonging to differing income brackets. This presents an enormous task for social planning. Should members of such diverse groups dwell together? If the answer is assumed to be affirmative, then at what level should the integration take place?

The government had to make a clear-cut decision, even at the risk of negative selection. With time, it became clear that the more active and independent inhabitants of an apartment house, neighbourhood or community leave, while the more passive remain and the unavoidable product would be an 'instant slum', a creation of public investment.

While adopting an integration policy, it was obvious that there was little hope for real integration within one generation. Nevertheless, it was decided that any public policy must have a practical target for, without practical action, polarisation between affluent and needy will grow. On the other hand, simplifications and 'slogan policies' might create even more chaos, more frustrations, more mutual suspicion and mistrust.

The policy of creating a maximum of 'meeting spots' is perhaps the best example in planning. Such a policy removes the necessity for apartment houses as a means of achieving degrees of integration. One common kindergarten or school, one joint playground, one chapter of any political party, one place of employment became the basis for establishing friendships and recognition; and in this programme social cohesion began. In such neighbourhood planning, inhabitants of differing backgrounds may live apart, keeping their own habits, but the youngsters and the children create the new society.

A 'separate' neighbourhood, created unintentionally, proved to be dangerous to the programme. It lacked the elements to encourage contact and social interchange. There, old habits were seldom supplemented; new values were adopted slowly. All the investment in social and cultural activities were in vain; while, on the other hand, social and cultural action in integrated neighbourhoods produced positive results.

There is agreement that housing is not a separate problem in itself. It is only a part of a complex socio-economic make-up. Housing should not be regarded as a mere technical tool, designed for providing a roof over people's heads. In the dynamics and reality of Israel, a nation with changing values and high individual mobility, a new society fundamentally different from the societies from which most of the Israelis came, a new neighbourhood or a new town is more than a number of housing units. This area was, and still is, one of the brightest opportunities to create a new and better integrated nation.

The present housing policy in Israel is the result of a twenty-year trial and error process. Since independence, one basic tenet has been maintained: every citizen, old and new, is entitled to assistance in finding an adequate shelter.

Adequate shelter is interpreted to mean minimum space with basic requirements for each household. What minimum space means remains an open question. Minimum standards at any given period reflect the level of any economy as a whole.

Permanent Housing Construction in Israel: Housing Units Completed, Average Size in sq. metres, and Sponsor, 1948–70

	Total		Public		Private	
	Units	Average space	Units	Average space	Units	Average space
1948–52	119,200	44·4	80,760	37·0	38,440	60·0
1953–56	111,075	56·6	76,640	48·0	34,435	76·0
1957–60	128,320	62·5	82,455	54·0	45,865	78·0
1961–63	104,330	67·4	61,270	55·0	43,060	85·0
1964–66	113,550	74·7	58,070	62·0	55,480	88·0
1967–69	76,300	83·1	31,140	72·0	45,160	93·0
1970	28,800	80·0	9,700	76·0	19,100	95·0
Total	681,575	75·5	400,035	65·4	281,540	85·0

In 1948 public housing in Israel began, based on the premise that thirty square metres was an adequate minimum space for a household. Today, seventy-two square metres are regarded as the minimum. Within twenty years, Israel has constructed 681,000 housing units; 400,000 financed by or with some assistance from the government, and 245,000 were built by private or corporate investment. Out of this relatively new housing stock there are some units, of course, regarded as substandard by today's standards.

Here the country faces another major problem. Raising of new housing standards is proper and inevitable as a function of a general rise in the standard of living. However, the problem of whether to improve the existing stock of housing or to devote attention to additional housing is crucial both from the social and political point of view.

Israel also has unusual problems in the area of architectural quality. Western immigrants, used to individualisation and a standard considerably higher than other immigrants, demand more, not only in space but in type of accommodation. The nation's architectural ingenuity is further strained by the need to consider the demands of a war economy, at a time when the more sophisticated demands of an important sector of the population with a contribution to make have to be considered. But recognition of the problem is, in part, helpful in meeting it, at least to the best of present ability. A cursory consideration of the housing built during the past ten years indicates a diversification from building to building, from project to project and from area to area, all part of efforts at meeting individual needs as much as possible.

Housing for new immigrants, new villages and new towns has received top priority in Israeli public housing. For many years all other housing needs were delayed. Little was accomplished in the field of slum clearance. The problems of young couples in the metropolitan areas, for example, got more considered attention only in 1971. In recent years a need to re-examine past policies in several fields has been recognised.

For several years, more attention has been given to the problem of slums, in both their social and economic aspects. The one consideration, among others, has been: should the slum population be transplanted, *en masse*, with its slum heritage and attitude, or should it be dispersed with its existing life-style, recognising the trauma, and sometimes persistent maladjustment in a new environment.

Another problem, in a society of limited resources, where the housing needs of the poorer portion of the population are the responsibility of the public bodies, is the need to develop a comprehensive renewal programme for the most dilapidated parts of the city. The question then becomes should such responsibility precede activities aimed at solving the housing problems of the most needy living in the most difficult conditions? Should, in other words, the approach be geographic or selective? Israel decided to attack both areas simultaneously.

In dealing with urban housing requirements, there is often a tendency to stress public needs as opposed to those of the individual. The private sector claims it can serve the individual better, cheaper, and without use of taxpayers' money. Even advocates of government-supported housing claim that the government does not pay enough attention to the needs of the individual or utilise sufficiently the experience and financial ability of the business community.

There should be no contradiction between the public need and that of the individual. The danger lies in developing a one-sided point of view. The individualistic approach to slum clearance, or to a development project, can raise social or legal problems, and yielding to an individual can snowball, making the whole project unworkable. Yet an approach to the problem can be worked out satisfactorily. Private business participation can be used more widely providing that the public interest is not forgotten. Although there is a judicial structure to guard the public interest, a watchful eye is needed, as no one is exempt from pressures and lobbying. For example, planning is, and should be, the sole responsibility of public bodies, while actual construction work should be decided in terms of the needs of each project with some being public and some being private. Any orthodoxy, in this area, can be harmful. The greatest harm arises when private enterprise or individual interest is given dominant consideration, as opposed to public enterprise and vice versa. The truth, as far as a small country is concerned, lies in close co-operation between the two elements.

The Israeli economy, in most fields, is a mixed one—state, public and private enterprise. State activities are limited to basic services and industries like power, air and sea transport, railways, material resources; private and public enterprises compete among themselves. Sometimes the government works with corporations to promote new activities. In other cases, shares in government corporations are sometimes sold partly, or fully, to private non-governmental corporations. There is no ideology or doctrine behind it but the approach simply reflects the need of a developing economy.

Housing is no exception to this interplay between various sectors of the country. While in some countries municipal bodies control the field of public housing, the national government takes their place in Israel. Sixty per cent of the housing units constructed in Israel were sponsored or initiated by government controlled bodies. Any housing programme or even a single housing unit, sold or rented to a private citizen and which was helped by governmental subsidy is regarded as public housing. Sometimes statistical data does not cover all the various government financing activities, especially in the field of loans to individual citizens and in the field of co-operatives. If these activities were included in the statistical data, the share of 'public' housing would be even larger.

There is no direct link between the citizen as customer and the government, namely the Ministry of Housing, as seller. Planning, ordering, supervision, financing and granting of individual loans is in the hands of the ministry, while the actual link with the citizen, as customer, is in the hands of other bodies.

In most cases it will be the Amidar corporation dealing with renting, selling and maintaining the housing property. Amidar is a governmental corporation responsible to and acting under ministry directives.

Amidar not only deals with the maintenance of housing, including all reparations and current upkeep, but also functions in community relations, welfare, general social work and co-operates with municipal bodies and other governmental agencies.

The relations between the inhabitants of Amidar property and the corporation bear no similarity to the so-called normal landlord-dweller relations. The most important facet of Amidar's work, in the social area, is in developing community life, local leadership and responsibility.

In many neighbourhoods the Amidar field office is the only official institution and the man on the spot, the sole representative of the Israeli establishment. His duties, responsibilities and concerns exceed, by far, his formal status as the local agent of the landlord.

The basic financing system has been that of direct government loans to tenant owners from budgetary sources. Loans and grants for proposed housing are included in the State Developmental budget. State loans from budgetary sources are generally granted at a rate of interest fluctuating between 7½ per cent and 9 per cent for a period of twenty-five to thirty years according to geographical and social priorities.

Additional means are supplied by the mortgage banks at government-regulated rates of interest. Loans and housing mortgages are executed by the mortgage banks, the biggest one being the Tphachoth bank, partly owned by the government.

Increasing housing needs and the heavy burden of defence budgets caused ever-growing difficulties in securing the needed minimal means. Although the housing budget is second only to defence, the total means available is still insufficient. An effort has been made to increase the place of private mortgage banks in financing of public housing. Thus a problem of rates of interest and redemption period has arisen. The usual terms of first mortgage loans for public housing purposes has been 8 per cent (plus 3 per cent insurance premium against depreciation in money value) with a ten- to fifteen-year redemption period. Second mortgage loans are given on a 4·5–6 per cent (plus 3 per cent insurance as above) for a period of twenty to thirty years.

The principle of providing more resources from the banking system was to equalise the terms of the additional loans through a state subsidy. Thus, with a I£45,000 sale or cost price, there is a I£7,500 down payment; a subsidised loan of I£27,500; and a 'Normal Banking System' loan of I£10,000. In fact currently, these subsidised banking system loans amount to 12 per cent of the total as compared with 4 per cent in 1970 and virtually none in 1969.

In connection with financing in Israel, the system of making the individual mortgage payment variable with the inflationary aspects of the economy must be mentioned. Under this system, mortgage loans are repaid in currency of equal purchasing power. While this system did elicit more money from capital sources, it was much less satisfactory to the borrowers.

Increasing the monthly payment in accordance with a type of cost of living index formula has slowed up the already lengthy repayment period and has contributed to the feeling of 'forced ownership'. From a purely economic point of view the link between the cost of living index and the mortgage instalments never closed the gap between the real decrease in money value and the real decrease in purchase property value. Still, popular feeling finally brought a change in policy and since 1966, 3–4 per cent cost of living link insurance has been added to the regular interest cost. Thus the monthly instalments, although higher than before, are fixed over the repayment period.

Method of Financing by Type of Recipient, by Source of Funds, by Average Amount 1971. (US $ = 4·2 I£.) (£ sterling = 10·73 I£).

Type of recipient	Average price of a flat	Down-Payment	State-Loan	Mortgage (Commercial loan)	Other Sources
			In Israeli £		
Immigrant Housing	50,000	10,000	30,000	10,000	—
Rural Housing	40,000	4,000	36,000	—	—
Young Couples	50,000	5–10,000	30–40,000	5–10,000	—
Development Areas	60,000	4–15,000	32–40,000	7–13,000	—
Slum Clearance	70,000	5–10,000	40–49,000	6–10,000	10,000
Popular Housing Schemes	60,000	40–43,000	5–10,000	10–12,000	—
Private Housing Schemes	85,000	70,000	—	15,000	—

The above figures are related to cases of purchase. Most of immigrant housing, a large part of slum clearance and housing in development areas are based upon rent-system.

Classification of Dwelling Property according to the Flat Holding System by Sponsor (1969)

Details	Total Number	Private	Public	Total	Private	Public
					(percentage)	
TOTAL number of families	681,400	307,830	373,570	100·0	45·1	54·9
Flats owned by occupants	416,130	217,830	198,300	100·0	52·3	47·7
Flats leased by public corporations	175,270	—	175,270	100·0	—	100·0
Flats leased by private landlords prior to 1953	90,000	90,000	0	100·0	100·0	—

While there are no great changes in the principle of the system of tenant ownership, there are more doubts than in the past and more voices against the principle.

The general ownership policy had a number of favourable influences on economic and social development. Primarily it made it possible to raise very substantial amounts for financing housing and constituted a stabilising factor for population movement. It also seemed to insure better maintenance of property. As we have seen, the down payment for public housing can amount (together with the normal bank first mortgage loan) to about 30 per cent of the total investment in public housing. It is difficult to imagine abandoning this source of financing equivalent to 7,000 housing units annually.

The second major advantage in the owner-occupier system is in respect of maintenance problems. It is believed that the more binding the attachment of an individual to his home, the better will be the up-keep of the property. The doubts, however, pile up.

Real ownership means real investment. Down payments of 15 per cent to 35 per cent are resented by the tenants who are reluctant to re-pay the loans they had to obtain to pay these, feeling that they are forced loans. On the other hand, when the down payment is only an insignificant percentage of the total it cannot be regarded as a real purchase. In many cases, the tenants regard the down payment as an unreasonable form of key money or government tax and monthly instalments as a kind of assessment which is unreasonably high or unfair; but with no real ownership feeling, there is no personal attachment to the property and hence no great incentive to maintain it well.

Dealing with less affluent members of the population, which is by definition the major duty of the public agencies, sometimes makes the owner-occupier system a mere fiction. These people are unable to provide a down payment of any significance or to take any responsibility for repayment of loans even at the lowest rates of interest and the longest amortisation schedules. In many cases, these are families with six or seven children dependent partially or wholly on social benefit incomes. It seems to us that in these cases, among others, public ownership and maintenance of property with a social rent at a rate related to family income is the only logical solution.

In the long run, public ownership makes tenant mobility easier and ensures that if, in the future, a need for removal arises due to unforeseen changes in land use or in general planning the price to be paid will not exceed the amount of money needed for alternative housing.

With the present system of low down payment, ownership only becomes a reality when it is necessary to move and then the price paid for the equity bears no relation to the value of the property or to the cost of alternative housing.

The present system of priorities represents both the *raison d'être* and the most urgent needs of Israel: housing for immigrants, continuous development of the southern and northern parts of the country, both the rural and urban areas, slum clearance and popular housing schemes.

Priorities are expressed in terms of eligibility, as well as in scope or terms of assistance. For example, in most remote parts of the country the settler is entitled to a rented flat, on a very liberal rent basis not withstanding his economic or social status, whereas the same settler in the metropolitan area is expected to purchase his flat with a down payment according to his economic ability. Even the terms of the loan will change with respect to interest rate and the number of years allowed to repay the loan. Also rents in the new buildings are reserved for difficult social problem cases. The only exception is the new immigrants who are entitled to a rented flat, wherever they are settled indicating the special priority given to their absorption in the country.

We cannot overlook the deficiencies in the priority system. Nevertheless, a programme without priorities means yielding to pressure groups, petty politicos, local party bosses and powerful individuals. On the other hand, consistent enforcement of rigid priorities produces unavoidable amounts of injustice and discontent. The political decision to give preference to certain groups and areas is not an easy one to handle in the field of housing.

Eighty-nine per cent of the total government expenditure on housing starting with 1965–6 was allotted to 30 per cent of the population. This meant that the needs of almost half a million families, out of the total 732,000, were to be satisfied by 11 per cent of the government expenditure on housing.

The present priorities system, while justified in terms of national and social goals, is under constant criticism and realignment. Finally in 1971 young couples secured sizeable assistance and recent inter-ministerial deliberations brought about some changes in this area without changing the basic principles of the present policy.

3

Twenty years' activity in housing is a long trial and error period. Much has been accomplished. About 1·2 million new immigrants were absorbed and a completely new Israel emerged in the process. Most of the remaining problems are not in the field of housing, nor in the field of social and economic development. Peace remains in the future and the Israeli citizen has had to pay the full price of his security. Many ideas had to be postponed. One thing should be stressed: there are worthy achievements in this country and all of them are in the field of human development. The story of Israel is really the story of creating a new nation and a new citizen consciously participating in the society and ready to take part in personal involvement and responsibilities.

Human development is definitely not a short-term effort. Development assumes continuity and this is being accomplished in spite of unfavourable external conditions. Housing was never regarded as a separate target in Israel. Rather, it is a prerequisite in attaining social aims and human development. There is no such thing as a zenith in education and health levels; there is no optimum in healthy family relations; there is no such quality as citizen pride, without proper housing. Therefore, even today, when so much is needed in other fields, the housing budget in Israel is second only to the need for security.

Chapter 5 Trade Union Housing in Western Germany

JOHANN WOLFGANG WERNER

Over the second half of the past century, the German labour movement faced the decisive question of whether to achieve the improvement of living conditions of broad segments of the population by evolutionary or revolutionary means. In the face of the enormous need for housing, sharp disputes developed concerning housing policies, particularly between Friedrich Engels and Sax, the reformer. The German trade unionists chose, at that time, a programme of reform, through the formation of workmen's housing co-operatives along with savings associations. Subsequently, the union activity helped to transform the housing co-operative movement into a housing reform movement with a view to improving the general welfare of the population.

To stimulate public interest, the Berlin Workmen's Health Commission published a report about housing conditions in Berlin in 1893. In 1901 the local health insurance fund for merchants, commercial clerks and pharmacists began an investigation of the health and housing of its members. Numerous health insurance funds and cities in Germany followed this example, continuing investigations regularly until 1920. Further investigations by city administrators indicated that intensive housing needs prevailed. The need was considerably increased by the First World War and the ensuing inflation.

By 1923, approximately 600,000 families had no housing at all and 100,000 more were in severely overcrowded dwellings. By 1927, housing experts indicated that more than a million dwellings were needed and in addition about 490,000 families lived in overcrowded buildings. Even these statistics did not reflect the actual extent of the housing need since an apartment with one room and kitchen was considered overcrowded only if occupied by more than four persons.

Despite these conditions the majority of the population, however, failed to understand the importance of the housing problem. Local politicians were largely dominated by property owners, who were the only eligible voters in most cities up to 1918. No elections were held in many rural communities, for example in the whole estate districts of Prussia. The strength of the interest groups in Parliament was reflected by the rejection of the housing laws submitted to the government by its legislative body. This legislative body had been elected on the basis of the *three classes voting right*. It was for this reason that German labour considered the attainment of general, equal and secret voting rights as an essential pre-condition for advancing their housing needs.

The unions demanded a long-term programme from the central government as well as from some individual states in order to eliminate the housing shortage. Under the programme profits derived from land speculation were to be 'skimmed off' by tax measures. It was further proposed that municipalities receive the legal right of first purchase for new construction land, and that salutary traffic conditions be provided in outlying regions because inexpensive construction land could still be bought in these areas.

After the First World War unions, as well as co-operatives, for the first time became seriously involved in meeting this increased housing need. The decisive breakthrough came about through non-profit companies, such as unions and co-operatives working for the general welfare of the population rather than merely for their own members. This point of view characterised the union approach which made it a point of principle to solve the overall problems of society in such a manner as to provide examples to other enterprises.

Activities of Unions

In 1919, to lower the cost of building, construction workers in Berlin and seventeen other cities founded the Association of Building Enterprises (VSB). The VSB was organised as an 'umbrella' organisation and stock company. Its purposes were to advise local *Bauhutten* organisations and to organise new branches. Boards of directors and Supervisory Boards were represented by union members. By 1922, twenty-seven branches, with more than 21,000 workers, were affiliated to the VSB. The VSB organisation was severely affected by inflation in the early years. It also suffered from insufficient professional and commercial leadership. As a result the number of local Bauhutten firms decreased to 173 in 1923 and eventually fell to 128 in 1929. Yet the average gross dollar volume per firm increased about

350 per cent between these years; and the total business increased from 41 million Reich marks to 137 million Reich marks. Up to 1929 VSB had built 82,000 apartment units and were known for their building quality. They also influenced working conditions and prices in a most positive way. VSB and some of its branches developed their own companies in the building material industry. By the end of 1929, they controlled twelve brickyards, four sawmills, four stone pits, four sand pits, three factories for fashioning wood and three concrete plants.

Two principal decisions proved to be landmarks for union involvement in large-scale home building. The first resulted from the decision of the congress of the German General Labour unions in Leipzig (ADGB) in 1922 when it founded its own labour building association. The association began by building apartments and housing estates, and lobbied for improvement in housing conditions.

The second was the decision of the eighth regular federal congress of the German unions in 1969, in Munich, to authorise Neue Heimat to operate actively in the planning of urban areas, including the development of regional housing policies and the planning and building of new towns. In both of these decisions the enlarged scope of unionised activity, especially in the field of housing reform and the development of better living conditions became apparent. If, in 1922 emergent housing need was the main concern, by 1969 the policies of planning for the future had taken over. Both led to the same goals: the raising of the standards of living of much of the population.

The decision of the ADGB in 1924, based on plans proposed by Martin Wagner, resulted in the founding of an organisation (DEWOG) whose function was to build good and inexpensive homes for workers, employees and civil servants. The initial capitalisation, 50,000 Reich marks ($12,500) was increased several times. When the capital support of the consumer co-operatives' insurance funds and the workers' bank fund, were added, total capital was 3 million Reich marks ($750,000). Up to the year 1932, however, DEOWG did virtually no building but limited itself to technical and financial promotion of building enterprises and establishing associations and societies throughout Germany.

Its extensive building activity began in the local union housing enterprises, such as in Berlin, with the affiliated company GEHAG which had been founded in 1924 by the free unions. Up to 1933 this group had built between 40,000 and 50,000 low-cost dwellings as model housing estates. At about the same time, other unions also created their own home building enterprises, as for example the Christian National Union in 1929. The large 'white collar' unions, particularly those of national structure, founded the GAGFAH Joint Stock Company in Berlin with an original capital of 2 million Reich marks. Its primary concern was housing reform and prevention of land speculation. By 1937 this organisation had built 53,000 dwellings; 31,000 of which were apartments and 22,000 private homes. Numerous smaller organisations were formed on a union basis. These organisations, particularly those founded by civil servants, worked together with building savings and loan funds, for example, Wustenrot, the oldest such fund in Germany (which had even then 35,000 members), to secure finance for their building activities. In addition to this building activity, the German unions remained actively in the field, pressing for housing policy reform. They fought for an appropriate housing law, progressive land policies and the extension of housing for families of low to moderate income. They also prompted state-aided housing and a law for building codes and regulation of construction that would also cover the management of existing buildings.

In 1926 the local union board of directors of Greater Hamburg and the General German Union (ADGB) founded GEKABE, a limited non-profit organisation, of Hamburg. This organisation by 1931 had completed about 2,500 dwellings in Hamburg. In 1933 GEKABE, along with other unionised property, was officially dissolved. In Germany as a whole, in spite of the many thousands of units built by unions, more than 50 per cent of the stock of such dwellings had been completely destroyed by the end of 1945. Most of the pre-war housing stock that managed to survive was severely damaged.

In 1945, GEKABE changed its name to Neue Heimat and all housing units were turned over to the surviving organisation. The new organisation assumed responsibility for construction of buildings and of housing estates, but the management was entrusted by the Allies to a trustee through decrees of control over the advisory committee. At the same time, some of the German unions which had been severely splintered founded the German Union Federation (DGB), while a segment established a separate federation of the employees, the German Employees Union (DAG). Up to 1949 there was not any co-ordinating organisation for West Germany and the structure of the unions was different in each of the three Western zones of occupation. In 1950 a federation of existing union housing enterprises was organised to co-ordinate all housing activity.

The first Neue Heimat association which was released by the trustee and turned over to the unions was Neue Heimat of Kassel. During the early 1950s, Heinrich Plett, manager of the Kassel Neue Heimat, had increased the activities and importance of his association through the reconstruction of the German mortgage loan market. When the new management of Neue Heimat began its work, with Heinrich Plett as president, and under the commercial leadership of Albert Vietor and the technical leadership of Walter Beyn, the development of the present overall organisation started. After some reorganisation and with new construction started on razed land and with the acquisition of new companies and the elimination of capital control through the Allies, Plett turned his attention to the mortgage loan needs of the organisation. The expansion of its activity beyond the city of Hamburg began in earnest. In May, 1950, the Hansa Building Association, also a limited responsibility company, was taken over and later developed into a regional association, Neue Heimat Nord. At the same time, and before the end of 1952, shares of AGEKA Hamburg, and partnerships in the GEWOG Hamburg and Wilhelmsburg were acquired.

In 1952 the union-examining board for the British zone decided to return the ownership of the shares of Neue Heimat, which had been under Allied trusteeship, to the trusteeship of the German union. The trustee advisory committee was changed into a supervisory board.

The decision by DGB in 1954 to invest the Neue Heimat association with the control of almost all newly returned, or newly acquired associations, and to raise their efficiency by this amalgamation, was an extremely important step. Neue Heimat-Hamburg, the most active company, became the holding association for the local groups and supervisory organisations were created in every federal state. Co-operation was assured by agreements reached between regional organisations and the co-ordinating organisation of Neue Heimat-Hamburg. The GEWOBAG association, a union non-profit housing company of Frankfurt, was the last association taken into

the Neue Heimat group in 1960. This group had twenty-seven
affiliated associations and a stock of 110,000 dwellings.

Three areas of operation must be considered which have bearing
on developments up to 1960: first, the repair and reconstruction of
partially demolished dwellings; new construction on bombed out
and burned out areas, according to the new plans; the building of
garden cities and housing estates in outer regions: and finally, the
removal of housing need within these functions. From the inception
of the local enterprise groups, the principle prevailed that the parent
association would assume only those functions which could be less
expensively and better handled centrally such as the provision of
financial means, the planning of typical buildings and other similar
responsibilities. Actual building activity, with all its preparatory
tasks remained the function of the regional and local organisations.
These local affiliates remained legally independent under their own
management. Even today, upwards of 80 per cent of Neue Heimat
employees are in regional offices, including that of Hamburg.

In 1957 the federal board of directors summarised its directives
for the work of the Neue Heimat Group and its housing principles
in its political guide lines as follows:

> The Federal Board of the associated German Labour unions of
> the DGB agreed upon the following maxims regarding housing
> policy:
>> The DGB shall make all efforts to eliminate the housing
>> shortage in order to realise for everyone his basic right to an
>> adequate dwelling in the near future.
>
> The non-profit housing enterprises have been ordered to
> increase the housing supply utilising the laws of public welfare
> and to provide cultural and social models for use elsewhere.
> Owing to the continuing housing shortage, an aggressive
> programme is still needed. Therefore, the DGB is to urge the
> government to pursue an active housing policy in accordance
> with social principles and to create the necessary legal,
> financial and economic conditions favourable for such
> building.

> *General Principles*
> Each individual has a legal claim to a dwelling up to certain
> moderate cultural standards to be guaranteed by the state;

the increasing living standards must be taken into consideration and existing dwellings that do not measure up to such standards must be replaced.

The dwelling size is determined by the number of household members.

Dwellings are to be priced at reasonable rents.

If the tenant is unable to pay this rent he should receive public subsidies for the difference, the amount depending upon income and family size. Public aid should be made available through monetary support to housing construction.

Methods of Removing the Shortage of Housing

The government must take all steps to overcome the housing shortage as soon as possible and should bring up measures serving this purpose with a general housing programme directed towards lower-income groups. At the same time consideration must be given to differing local needs and priorities must be established.

Federal districts and local communities must assume that housing construction is carried out according to modern housing construction rules and must provide suitable building sites.

Housing construction in already populated areas has to be achieved; primarily in the form of garden and town estates.

Traffic and developmental measures, as well as construction of public schools, hospitals, community centres and churches are to be financed by a special programme.

Building land has to be made available and leased at reasonable prices using legal steps to avoid speculative practices.

Financing of the overall development programme must be assured by measures that take into consideration the capital market and priorities must be established with respect to distribution of public means within the terms of the governmental budget.

Community facilities, such as kindergartens and playgrounds, are to be included as part of the programme.

To meet the people's housing need, research towards improved social or hygienic ends has to be pursued along with maintaining flexibility in construction and housing requirements.

Creation of segregated housing with respect to special income

3*

or professional groups, including so-called 'company dwellings', must be avoided.

Realisation of the housing programme is urgent, in comparison with other building programmes.

Advancement of the programme can only proceed through reasonable administrative measures, and rigid housing regulations are, wherever possible, to be avoided.

Families with children and people living in deteriorated housing are to receive preferential treatment in the form of rents and subsidies.

Non-profit enterprises, such as co-operative societies and private eleemosynary efforts following the rules of welfare are also to receive first consideration.

Methods to Increase Dwelling Standards

After the elimination of the housing shortage, the existing stock of dwellings for old people has to be modernised in order to provide an adequate housing level for this population group. Legal obstructions, such as laws concerning building land and construction, must be eliminated.

New housing estates should be separated from industrial areas in such a way as to avoid interference with noxious odours, noises, or harmful elements such as poor traffic patterns. Sufficient secondary installations such as green belts, playgrounds, etc., are to be created.

Finally, legal tenant protection must be maintained and must become part of a general social legal framework.

As early as 1961 Neue Heimat looked for ways to expand from the building of homes to the broader functions of urban renewal and planning. This expanded activity included planning and building, simultaneously with industrial projects, supermarkets and other community facilities. The inadequate supply of community facilities —libraries, schools, hospitals, shopping centres—proved to be one of the greatest obstacles in meeting ideals of the unions for balanced living conditions. The shortage of governmental investment capital together with the task of establishing building priorities made comprehensive planning very difficult. It was made equally difficult by the restrictive laws on non-profit housing, which permitted the associations to provide housing projects for broad levels of the population as well as some specific additional facilities such as central laundries and playgrounds but did not allow them to engage in urban reconstruction and town planning in a comprehensive manner.

In 1962, the Neue Heimat Group worked out a co-operative arrangement with a private industrial building company, Gewerbebautrager GmbH, where the private organisation assumed the responsibility for the development of shopping centres. During the ensuing years a number of shopping centres in the Hamburg area, in the Frankfurt area and other places have been developed by this organisation. A secondary school and a department store in Elbe were other similar ventures.

In 1962, Neue Heimat International was established with the aim of communicating the experiences of Neue Heimat to foreign nations and in order to take an active part in establishing a common European housing and building market. The financing of Neue Heimat International is derived from the union and, to a considerable extent, from the other countries. In Vienna there is 100 per cent financing by Neue Heimat but in several other countries in Europe Neue Heimat has only a 50 per cent interest and in the trans-Atlantic countries, 33 per cent.

Special funds were necessary to finance the establishment of Neue Heimat International. Financial policies of Neue Heimat had to be considered in terms of the international sector, to avoid risks in monetary exchange rates. For this reason, Neue Heimat operates in Europe and other continents in conjunction with a number of foreign credit institutions which assumed the financing of construction in the countries co-operating in the programme. For the first time, through this programme, German credit institutions provide mortgages for construction, outside the Federal Republic, within the framework of the European Common Market.

After the death of Heinrich Plett, in 1963, Vietor took over the presidency of Neue Heimat. Vietor was determined to extend Neue Heimat in the area of urban planning and renewal and to break through the restrictiveness of the laws regarding non-profit housing. He also stimulated original methods for bringing about housing reform and tackling more comprehensive tasks.

In 1963 Neue Heimat founded a research organisation for housing and urban planning, GEWOS, whose function was basic research concerning area planning, regional development, reconstruction of cities and the development of the necessary scientific tools and methods of investigating market structure, structural analysis and structural processes for builders. This market analysis was particularly important because while the housing shortage has been greatly alleviated with 20 million dwellings, many of them new, provided for 60 million people since the war, many sections of the population are still not adequately served and the aim of such analysis is to pinpoint where the housing is most needed. At the same time the task is to find ways to improve the present housing standards. By the beginning of 1971, GEWOS had a full-time staff of thirty professionals and more than 200 professors and experts as advisors in various special fields.

In 1963 after the occupancy of the 200,000th dwelling unit of Neue Heimat, Vietor announced that NH was to become the instrument for urban reconstruction and regional policy of the German unions. In 1964, as a follow up to this procedure, Neue Heimat Kommunal, a non-profit corporation whose function is the development of community buildings such as libraries, university buildings, hospitals, kindergartens, community centres, etc., was founded as an affiliated company. In one recent year, Neue Heimat Kommunal reported working on thirteen hospitals, three homes for hospital nurses, twenty schools, nine kindergartens and youth hostels, twelve nursing homes for the elderly and one university expansion project.

In 1969 German unions reaffirmed their programme concerning space planning, regional development and urban reconstruction, at the eighth federal congress of DGB, and commissioned Neue Heimat to continue to work towards the fulfilment of the objectives. Correspondingly, the power of Neue Heimat was enlarged in the following months. Neue Heimat Staedtbau (NHS) was founded by the unions in 1969 with a basic capital of 10 million Deutsche marks ($3 million), a new holding company for the non-housing building functions of the Neue Heimat Group. In September, 1969, NHS founded, along with a private corporation for the development of industrial enterprises, GIA, the sponsors of which were not only Neue Heimat but four large German banks: Bank für Gemeinwirtschaft, Commerzbank, Deutsche Bank and the Dresdener Bank.

Since 1969, organisations responsible for developing research, shopping centres and industrial factories can call upon a complete range of facilities in the fulfilment of urban projects; and these facilities have become an important adjunct to the federal and local governments in the field of home building, home management, city sanitation, city expansion, and development of cities. The integrated urban reconstruction which should be the aim and task of the political builder, can now be carried out to a far better degree by these organisations, in partnership with municipalities, than in earlier years.

Actually Neue Heimat Group engages in the following activities:

1. Basic research concerning city building.
2. Structural analysis by region and structural prognosis as well as market research by GEWOS.
3. Advice on regional and local developmental programmes including the following areas:
   (a) Home building
   (b) Community building
   (c) Building of industrial commercial institutions
   (d) Industrial developments.

As part of these responsibilities the following functions are in whole, or part, performed for local areas:

1. Focusing the programme
2. Planning
3. Acquisition of lots
4. Co-ordinating distribution and the awarding of contracts
5. Financial support
6. Supervision of building
7. Renting, selling, leasing, administering and managing.

This wide group of services offered by the Neue Heimat Group including its own as well as foreign specialists, such as architects, planners, estimators and so on, can be utilised by private builders, by business enterprises, both smaller or larger communities and by individual states or the federal government.

By the end of 1972, and since the beginning of its programme, Neue Heimat had completed almost 390,000 homes and industrial units for more than one million people in the federal republic of Germany. Almost 290,000 homes and industrial units were under its own administration. It also built over 130,000 small individual dwellings for ownership. Total building activity and administration reached a 4·2 billion DM investment in 1972 and about 3·1 billion were devoted to housing investments. Its growth may also be appreciated from the fact that in 1950 only 30 million DM were involved, but by the end of 1971 the amount reached 10·8 billion. The number of employees in Neue Heimat rose from 124 to 4,908 in the same period.

In all, housing benefiting from public funds (which is called 'Social Housing') constitutes about 227,000 units annually, or 40 per cent of the total housing production of Germany. Neue Heimat provides about one-sixth of this. These units include housing built by all co-operatives, by municipalities, and a substantial number of homes built for private home ownership. Neue Heimat alone provides about one out of five of its units for private home ownership.

The companies of Neue Heimat received their initial capital from the German unions during the first years of their development. It is important to recognise that although the Neue Heimat board is controlled through the unions, through the policies of the board of directors, it also has to operate under competitive conditions of the market as far as its achievements are concerned.*

Up to 1950, dwellings for low-income families built by Neue Heimat as social housing were financed by the government, except for the equity. Because of scarce public funds the production of such housing was limited. In Kassel, Heinrich Plett had already begun to obtain capital from private markets and to increase the volume of such financing most successfully and he and Vietor emphasised these policies when they took over the management of Neue Heimat. They were prepared to accept market conditions for mortgage deals and began to develop new forms of financing. In co-operation with numerous private and public land credit institutions, Neue Heimat arranged for the sale of deeds and community obligations at prices corresponding to the market, but the interest fluctuated on these bonds. In those years the much discussed 'grey market', the market with real prices, originated. These realistic market practices enabled mortgage institutions to dispose of numerous mortgages by buying bonds through Neue Heimat. Since this period, close co-operation has existed between most of the German mortgage institutions and Neue Heimat. Through this method of tapping private funds, many new possibilities were opened for the entire field of building low-cost housing—possibilities without which the miracle of building more than 10½ million new homes in Germany, in the years 1950 to 1970, might not have been possible.

* The unions, as entities, allow the professional staff at NH considerable, if not complete freedom and latitude in making their professional and business decisions regarding the quantity, locations, type and cost of housing.

The typical German financing of home building consists of a first mortgage and a second mortgage, with the financing of the equity from one's own money, loans from an employer or public means. Neue Heimat succeeded in attracting capital funds, to a large extent in the area of second mortgage loans for which government guarantees could be arranged. It arranged for the sale of public obligations at market prices and enabled the mortgage institutions to set sale prices with second mortgages included. Various cities have assumed the responsibility of guaranteeing these loans, as well as helping with the respective payments of interest and principal so that rents could be maintained. This meant that the federal government was relieved of some of the loans because private or local public money was substituted and the volume of private production was at the same time increased enormously. Hamburg, Schleswig-Holstein and Hesse, as well as a number of other large cities used this method to make possible large programmes of home building and at the same time, encourage the general growth of the German economy. The new system for financing became official policy through the Second Law for building homes.

A further source for the financing of home building by Neue Heimat resulted from the use of Paragraph 7-C in the income tax law. This section enabled industry to grant employee mortgage loans for building homes and to deduct all or part of these amounts from taxable incomes according to an agreed scheme. These 7-C funds were considered as substitutes for second mortgages and were guaranteed by the government helping to pay the annuities of interest and amortisation. Neue Heimat succeeded in raising almost 500,000,000 DM (more than 10,000 units) under these 7-C mortgages. All the houses were purchased by low-income families under this procedure. Special financial arrangements made it possible to function by liquidating the existing mortgages and to expand other mortgage commitments and these income tax subsidies were also used for stimulating reconstruction of destroyed areas. In 1953, Neue Heimat, without resorting to public mortgages but by utilising 7-C, built the garden city of Hamburg-Hohnercamp with almost 1,600 dwellings. The rent, at that time, amounting to 1·65 DM per square metre, in relation to present rentals for apartments of 6 to 8 DM per square metre, was extraordinarily low. Actually present rentals are even higher because the average number of square metres per apartment has been substantially increased. By 1956, Neue

Heimat were engaged in large programmes of building for private ownership for families of skilled workers. Nine thousand private homes were built in the late fifties in the federal republic and many more subsequently, again utilising 7-C.

To keep the costs to the buyers as low as possible other financial arrangements were introduced. A third mortgage requiring only a down payment of 15-20 per cent was instituted for those people who had little capital but could afford greater monthly payments because of a growing monthly income. Many of these people also received additional aids from the government reducing their 'out of pocket' costs substantially.

The liberalised land market in the Federal Republic, plus the far-sighted land provisions made under the Federal law, became among the most essential preconditions for long-term building programmes and favourable production costs. All in all, one of the great problems Neue Heimat faces in providing low-cost housing is the problem of land cost. Without an adequate supply of land, at reasonable prices, the modernisation of towns and improvement of housing is not possible. Generally speaking, the co-operative sector of the market, including Neue Heimat, buys land at prices about 30 per cent below that of the private sector. Most of this difference lies in the question of timing and placement of such land. At the present time, there is a proposal in Parliament to allow co-operatives to buy land at below market prices.

However, even with good land costs, building costs have climbed so steeply that despite all the general subsidies to construction, from government as well as the 7-C inducements, and despite the advantages of the non-profit arrangements of the co-operatives, such as Neue Heimat, rentals are well above what low-income wage earners can afford. Hence the government's individual subsidy has been, and is, necessary in order that the wage earner pay a reasonable part of his income in rent.

At the present time, on average, about 11-15 per cent of income is paid by tenants in rent. This, however, includes many people living in controlled rental units in government or co-operative housing or in older housing which does not possess all the amenities. In newer housing, percentages paid in rent go up to 15 per cent to 18 per cent, and many families who have to go into a new private housing market pay up to 30 per cent or higher.

The subsidies that are paid to the tenants, or private purchasers of low-cost housing, and which come under the term social housing, vary with the size and type of the family, the amount of family income and the amount of rent to be paid.

Since 1 January 1971, a new subsidy law has been, in effect, amending the 1965 law. Subsidies are grants paid by the government to tenants or private owners in order to cut the costs of rent or home-ownership. Every German citizen who cannot afford to pay the full rent or mortgage for adequate housing has a legal claim on such subsidies. The amount of subsidies varies with size of family, amount of family income and amount of housing expenditures. 800 DM per month is the ceiling for a single person, plus 200 DM for each family member. The family income is the sum of gross-income less deductions with a claim on subsidies as follows:

Number of family-members	Net family income DM	Gross income DM
One	800	1000
Two	1000	1297
Three	1200	1547
Four	1400	1822
Five	1600	2132
Six	1800	2442
Seven	2000	2762
Eight	2200	3082

Subsidies can be received for old and new dwellings, for publicly aided (in low cost housing), promoted by tax-allowances, or privately financed housing. Rents are not allowed to exceed a certain price level per square metre, i.e., rent subsidies are granted up to these rent ceilings only and rents exceeding this set maximum have to be paid wholly by the tenants themselves. The rent ceilings vary with areas (e.g. urban or rural) as well as amenities. Three examples of typical subsidies follow.

A pensioner and his wife live in an old home (without heating and bathroom) in a city of 1,000,000 inhabitants.

Old-age pension	550 DM
less 20 per cent general allowance	110 ,,
family income	440 ,,
rent per month	145 ,,
ceiling set by government	130 ,,
monthly subsidy according to schedule	56 ,,

Father, mother, two children (father only wage earner) lived in a newly built home (completed in 1971) provided with heating and bathroom, the home located in a city of less than 100,000 inhabitants.

Total income	1,435 DM
less allowance for 2nd child	25 ,,
less professional outlay	70 ,,
	1,340 ,,
less 20 per cent general allowance	268 ,,
	1,072 ,,
rent per month	320 ,,
ceiling rent set by government	310 ,,
subsidy per month	72 ,,

Father, mother and four children (father and one son are wage earners) live in a private house (built in 1965) provided with central heating and a bathroom, in a city of 300,000 inhabitants.

Gross income	2,010 DM
allowances for children	85 ,,
	1,925 ,,
general deduction	385 ,,
family income per month	1,540 ,,
monthly expenses for housing (interest and amortisation)	463 ,,
ceiling amount	383 ,,
monthly subsidy according to schedule	75 ,,

Public and private savings associations for buildings have for many years operated in their respective areas as partners with Neue Heimat. In co-operation with Neue Heimat Kommunal, special financial arrangements have been worked out with the state of Lower Saxony to finance their university programme. The total financing programme amounting to 971,000,000 marks was worked out by Neue Heimat in co-operation with a number of German credit institutions. The financing of schools and other public buildings are in fact among the ordinary transactions of Neue Heimat.

A real estate fund company was also founded together with the German mortgage deed institutions to help further financing objectives with industrial and home building. This fund is operated by selling small parcels, 'letters of home ownership', to broad levels of the population thus enabling them to acquire shares which are constant in value and which bear a good interest rate.

New and special solutions of financing are required in the industrial area. Financing shopping centres, hotels and similar institutions are such examples. Today Neue Heimat provides the financing for many regional development programmes. It is one of the largest factors of the German capital market with an annual need for investment of 1·3 billion DM.

Through the centralisation as well as the professionalisation of planning, Neue Heimat has been able to attract the most highly qualified architects for its buildings and has gained the acceptance of many municipal planning authorities. The group has been able to place planning experts at the disposal of local authorities in emergency situations and make it possible to start and carry through large construction projects in record time.

The efficiency of this group is further substantiated by the great number of city departments in Germany which have requested the assistance of Neue Heimat with zoning, planning and urban renewal, even though Neue Heimat actually built only a small proportion of the homes out of its own financial resources. The new urban district of Munich-Perlach, with about 25,000 homes, industrial and public establishments with 80,000 people, is one good example of this activity. Here Neue Heimat performed general planning and zoning functions along with the city of Munich in a manner which brought a great deal of credit to both participants.

Neue Heimat has, in fact, been a pace-maker with regard to such new town construction. More than ninety large housing complexes with 1,000 to 25,000 homes, have involved Neue Heimat. Not all of these are finished yet and some others are still in the planning stage. Increased attention is directed towards improving transportation and communication. Through the revitalisation of the inner cities and the creation of new nucleus communities with a market area of between 40,000 to 50,000 people, most of them living in rural districts, it attempts to make available to all citizens public and private housing services at reasonable costs aimed at the lower-income sector of the population.

In its programme for building, whether large housing complexes or new towns, Neue Heimat, while it believed that special consideration should be given to the weaker or poorer segments of society, believes that no segregation by groups is desirable or economically advantageous. At the beginning of its programme, Neue Heimat did concentrate on the poorer segment of society but with the development of a comprehensive programme and particularly as building costs have risen making good housing unavailable through the private sector to people of moderate means, Neue Heimat has recognised the need for a totally balanced programme.

The large building projects made it necessary early in the building programme to rationalise the construction process and Neue Heimat took advantage of this with pre-fabrication techniques. For many years not less than 40 per cent of all buildings have been built with prefabricated parts and on-site construction.

The centralisation of the administration made it possible to transfer the entire accounting records, including rent charging and other such functions, to the central office where a large computer, IBM 360–30, is located as part of the modern system of management and information. This modern electronic computation of data was used subsequently to analyse market structure and to execute construction plans according to the system of modern planning technology. Such facilities make it increasingly possible to offer housing at prices and time limits agreed upon. It must be emphasised that in spite of the massive central data collection programme, retaining local responsibility for administration with the holding company has been a decisive factor in the success of the whole enterprise.

The general policies of the enterprise, nevertheless, remain under the control of the executive board, which has six members and determines plans and decisions while the board of managers, which has fifteen members acts as a body to carry out these plans and decisions.

The unions demand control of economic power where they operate and this policy, pertaining to Neue Heimat, was fulfilled through the following controls:

(1) Through statutory regulations under governmental supervisory authorities, the statutes provide:
  (A) There is a duty to build standard homes for broad levels of population.
  (B) A maximum of 4 per cent return on investment to unions.
  (C) In the event the company is dissolved, stockholders (union) get no more than their paid up basic capital and the remaining assets are to be used for government purposes, in accordance with the statute.
  (D) To rent or sell such housing at levels to cover the basic costs with the analysis of cost being established by set regulations.
(2) Testing of management by various organisations of non-profit housing associations.
(3) Supervisory counselling boards in every local company must contain local union members. Local and overall holding companies must use representatives of the federal board of directors of DGB as well as representatives of union districts and individual unions in the regional groups.
(4) Appointment of managers and department heads are to be made by such supervisory boards.

The policies of the Neue Heimat proposed by management are discussed and decided upon in the boards of supervisory counsellors. In this way, constant co-ordination is maintained between interests of the unions and demands of the enterprise: consequently the interests of the employees go beyond the local builder organisation and are watched over by the members of the union on the boards of supervisory counsellors.

Companies of the Neue Heimat Group work together with other co-operative enterprises and especially with the business enterprises of the unions such as the union bank and its affiliates, the life insurance and property insurance companies of the unions and the consumer co-operative organisations. These sister companies do not, however, receive any favourable treatment in business transactions because Neue Heimat accepts the best offers available from the market place in order to keep rents or sale prices reasonable in their building activities, be it for apartments, private homes, offices or industrial buildings. Neue Heimat has made an important contribution to the economy, to urban design, to architecture, and to the infrastructure of German society. Neue Heimat has not only added to the dwelling unit supply, it has added a considerable measure to the amenities. It has provided for the management of housing stock; technical, financial and custodial services for small builders; served as a builder and seller of small homes for private ownership; builder of communal facilities such as schools, libraries and hospitals.

It may well be that a primary factor in its success is that although it has a union orientation it is completely community minded. This has been reaffirmed time and again through the extensive use made of Neue Heimat services by individual local communities.

Both the public and non-profit private organisations involved in housing are enormously important to the successful functioning of the private enterprise system in Germany. They serve on the one hand as a corrective factor by building at competitive prices and by setting their prices at such levels as to aim at the lowering of the general price level. In the course of setting this price, consumers gain by having balanced markets. For this reason it is the general policy of the Neue Heimat Group to lower prices by producing a surplus of housing and, in essence, force the withdrawal of bad housing from the market. In this aspect, housing reforms are made possible. It is correct to say that the provision of its housing, at below the rents allowable by government regulation, is one of the most significant contributions of Neue Heimat to the housing economy.

By long-term building programmes Neue Heimat hopes to support the continuity of construction by softening the cyclical waves of the construction market and to help the building industry pursue investment policies that are good for the total economy.

Neue Heimat makes possible the production and sale of larger volume of building parts, by greater standardisation, and encourages more favourable pricing structure. It also furthers technical progress with an extensive use of new building materials.

It engages in measures that contribute to the improvement of the structure of the economy and works to secure an upgrading of living standards in the population; and it serves as a catalyst to progress, productivity and creation of a healthy environment.

Neue Heimat continues to encourage the co-operation of all its local constituent companies to enlarge and expand its achievements. It considers itself the instrument of the unionised policies of society as well as the partner and servant of the government.

Chapter 6   The Co-operative Movement in Danish Housing

JOHN APELROTH

In 1967 when the joint organisation of the Co-operative Housing Society and the Public Social Housing Society had been functioning for fifty years, the non-profit housing development movement set a new record by completing 12,027 housing units. In 1969, one out of every four dwellings erected in Denmark was built without thought for any financial gain. Within the metropolitan areas, three out of every ten units were built for rental by co-operatives. The motivation behind this building movement is that the family must be able to obtain the best possible housing at the lowest possible price.

The 1969 record of housing units built is a milestone in the history of the non-profit community housing which was begun a hundred years ago in Denmark. The quarter of a century following the end of the Second World War has been a period of dynamic development as the number of units in this housing has multiplied tenfold, from 20,500 existing units in 1945 to over 250,000 units at the beginning of 1973. More than one million of the 5 million Danes live in non-profit housing, half of which was built by co-operative enterprises while the other half was built by housing societies headed by people chosen jointly by local government and by the occupants themselves. Of the one million, 45 per cent live in housing built in the Copenhagen area, 40 per cent in the Jutland area, about 10 per cent in the Seeland area outside Copenhagen, and 5 per cent in the Fuen area.

No matter how the boards may be composed, rent is determined by the cost of building and the administration. This principle has been fundamental to non-profit community housing in Denmark ever since the first slow start in the middle of the nineteenth century. At that time an epidemic of cholera raged in Copenhagen, taking thousands of lives. The physicians decided that one reason for the severity and the violent spread of the disease was the bad housing conditions in which the working class population was forced to live.

Part of the money collected by the Medical Association to help the needy was used in 1857 to start the Medical Association's first housing project, a project which even today, is characterised by its tenants as environmentally ideal, though the local government now wants to clear the area to develop split level houses and a bitter fight is in progress about the fate of this first housing project. From its beginning in 1857, the project was of a social character and quickly developed certain conveniences such as a shopping centre with a co-operative grocery store, a library, community centre and a nursery with green areas and small gardens. Today, these service facilities, as well as schools, common laundries, family rooms, and other community facilities are employed in every non-profit building project in Denmark.

The real emphasis in Danish building co-operatives began a few years later, in 1865, when some workers from the large shipyard, Burmeister, in Copenhagen, took the initiative to establish a workers' building association. This association never became of any great practical importance but it focused public attention on the enormous need for better housing for the lower classes. The association also built apartment buildings, some of which still exist but will soon be demolished by the present urban renewal programme of Copenhagen. These early efforts by the workers stimulated the legislature to be concerned with housing as early as 1887. A government loan bill was passed to permit loans from the state government to local governments or to building associations that built low-rent housing. According to the provisions of the bill, any profits derived from such housing were to be used to extend the programme of the building association, a principle still in effect today. Although the idea behind the bill was sound, the results were not startling because there was too little capital available to fund the programme and because of financial speculation. Then, as now, land and real estate values increased sharply so that in some cases the people who backed the building projects were able to repay the government loans and sell the houses, pocketing considerable profit.

These first co-operative and community housing projects did not really achieve much importance for lower-class people. The legislation itself simply did not make that possible and the workers who might have been interested in the co-operative idea were not able to amass even the modest down-payment to purchase the housing. Nevertheless, these houses must be considered monuments to the co-operative endeavours which underlie the present movement since they created good homes for families with limited means.

It was the private builders who built the housing for the workers in the big cities in Denmark and their work is still deplorably visible. The areas where housing dates from the 1900 period have the most serious slum problems today. The apartments in these buildings are small; most of them consist of two rooms and a kitchen, often using a common toilet with other tenants. They are far from ideal and presaged the start of non-profit community housing. Many of them are fire traps with their apartments opening off corridors that run down the middle of the house and with only one exit served by a wooden staircase. Production of such houses, bad as they were, ran completely wild and ended in an economic crash. During this period, there were 10,000 apartments available in Copenhagen. Yet the crash had such an effect on the employment of construction workers that it became necessary to reconsider the whole question of the co-operative building movement both as a means to stimulate the industry and as a means for providing housing for workers. A leader in this effort was the president of the union of building-carpenters in Copenhagen, J. Chr. Jensen.

Through him the Workers' Co-operative Housing Association was established in 1912. It is today the largest builder of social housing, responsible for 13,000 units. Next to it comes the Workers' Co-operative Building Association established in 1913, with 8,000 units. But the establishment of the Workers' Co-operative Housing Association became more significant because its operations became a model for similar associations in cities all over Denmark.

The lack of apartments was keen during and just after the First World War when most private builders pulled out of this form of investment. The government then moved in and granted loans to local communities and housing associations, until 1927 when it again became good business to build housing. Then public support for the co-operative movement lagged again when at the same time economic difficulties began to develop which led to a world-wide economic breakdown. Nevertheless, the members of the co-operative housing societies remained together through these years of crisis (1927–33) and the societies were later able to resume their building activity with renewed energy.

The modern development of these housing associations started when the government resumed granting loans for building of houses in 1933 to local governments and housing associations whose by-laws had to be approved by the Ministry of the Interior. This resulted in a re-organisation of the co-operative building movement. The most important rule then and now was that all the profits of an association must be spent either on new building projects or for modernising older housing. This was the beginning of the self-financing principle which today enables the housing movement to invest in the future through purchase of land and development of utilities.

The Act of 1933 expired in 1936, and for several years the government did not grant loans for housing projects. In 1938 a new Act was passed which provided for rent subsidies for large families, stimulated the establishment of social housing enterprises, especially among housing societies, and made loans possible for children's institutions, community centres and other developments of a social or cultural character. The Second World War brought building activity to an end and not until the end of the war, in 1945, was it possible to plan future activity based on the view that the whole question of housing was a problem for the community to solve. The need for housing during the war increased enormously and even during the twenty-five years since the end of the war, not enough housing has been built so that everyone, whether family or single person, can have the housing of his choice.

At the beginning of the Second World War the Minister of the Interior appointed a committee to study the housing problem, but its recommendations were not announced until after the war ended. These recommendations have provided the basic guide-lines for the social housing movement for the past twenty-five years. They stressed that the main objective of the social building movement is to provide good dwellings for the lower-income groups of the population at a rent they can afford. Secondly, when the building movement achieves sufficient financial stability, it can influence the general level of rents. The committee also stressed that legislation supporting the non-profit community housing should be of a more permanent and long-term character. For example, ten years was suggested as a possible period for legislation to be effective because of the need to take advantage of new technical developments and new types of housing.

While the co-operative movement does build primarily for members of its own group, membership is hardly exclusive and if all the flats are not rented by the members they are available to the general public. However, annual income must normally be below 50,000 krona and before taking a flat a family must become a member.

The non-profit community housing in Denmark is able to operate on a larger scale than private builders. They are also more able, and willing, to plan developments in accordance with total city plans, including necessary communal facilities. Most housing consists of three-storey buildings with only a small percentage of housing set apart for high-rise and these for small families and elderly. This housing is therefore of particular importance to larger family units although the average family size is fairly small in Denmark.

The non-profit community housing has lived up to its objective, especially through the joint organisation of the public housing societies which have come into existence within the recent past. Through meetings of this organisation there has been an exchange of information, increased co-operation, management courses have been offered, productive discussions have been held about the housing legislation which is frequently changed. 'We don't build for the present but for the future' is the organisation's motto.

New dwellings are expensive during the early years of their existence because of inflation and the tendency towards constant improvement but higher wages in the economy have so far counterbalanced this. Contributing to this counterbalance are the subsidised rents by income groups based on an agreement reached among the four largest political parties which will be effective for an eight-year period. This agreement was reached in 1966 and was intended to stabilise the conditions of the housing market. Individual subsidies are granted through a graded rent programme, with food allowances for single persons and for families with total annual income up to 60,000 krona ($8,400). The amount of the subsidy is determined by the relationship between the size of the apartment and the number of family members and their income.

These rent subsidies are available for various rental flats—new and old—private and non-profit. To receive a subsidy the tenant must apply and the home must be of a reasonable standard. The subsidy varies with the number of children in the family and the annual income. The more children and the less income the higher the subsidy. If for example the tenant pays an annual rent of 9,000 krona—with annual taxable income of 30,000 krona—and has a four-person family, the subsidy is 4,560 krona or about half of the rent.

There are some limits. Subsidies are reduced if the apartment is too large relative to family size and is not normally granted where the families occupy overcrowded facilities.

This subsidised rent allotment makes it possible for large families, with limited income, to move into new housing. The non-profit organisation constantly attempts to align the allotment within the inflation increase.

The political housing agreement for non-profit housing set a quota of 12,000 units per year. This 12,000 represents around 25 per cent of all the housing built in Denmark during the year, at a guaranteed interest of 5½–6 per cent for six years. This guaranteed interest is only available to non-profit community housing. The financing of the non-profit community housing is based on a down payment by the tenant of 6 per cent of the cost of the apartment, but only 3 per cent for housing started in 1972 or later. If the tenant's financial circumstances justify it, he can get a loan, or a guarantee for a loan, from the local government for part of the down payment.

For example, financial assistance towards down payments may be made available to all families where taxable incomes are less than 21,000–35,000 krona after deductions for children. If the income is more than 35,000 krona and the family lives in a standard house, or if their low income is of a temporary nature no assistance towards down payments can be made.

Repayment on these down payment loans is also very lenient. During the first five years unless his income has increased the tenant may arrange to pay nothing back. After that he may get several extensions and finally have ten years in which to pay off the loan.

Loans covering the remaining cost of the apartment are usually granted through three mortgage institutions, with government guarantees between 65 per cent and 94 per cent and up to 97 per cent of the value of the apartment. The mortgage societies get their money for loans by selling bonds on the open market. At present the interest yield on such bonds is between 10 per cent and 12 per cent. The government provides considerable support for the social, non-profit community and co-operative housing by granting subsidies equivalent to the difference between actual 10–12 per cent interest and the guaranteed interest of 5½–6 per cent. This subsidy is regarded as a temporary measure. After six years, according to present projections, it will be decreased gradually, by 16–25 per cent of the amount a year. After that, the tenant will have to pay full payment and interest on mortgages.

The housing agreement did bring a temporary stability to non-profit community housing. But the economic problems that have occurred add a tension aimed in the opposite direction. Land and interest rates have increased during the last twenty years so that the purchase price for a normal family dwelling has quadrupled (around 150,000 to 200,000 krona or $20,000–$30,000) and more than half of the increase is due to the enormous increase in interest costs. The cost of land has increased ten times while increases in the cost of materials and in labour has also resulted in higher costs for housing. Rental costs have increased five-fold during the last twenty years. Only because of the subsidised rent, the guaranteed interest arrangement and the non-profit housing arrangements has it been possible for families with average incomes to move into the new housing. Indeed, because of these arrangements, the non-profit community will be able to add 12,000 new units a year for years to come.

With 28 per cent of the population in the Copenhagen metropolitan area, the co-operative programme has 45 per cent of its housing stock in that city. In the early years of the current programme, half of the 12,000 units built annually by the co-ops were in Copenhagen. In the last several years, two out of three units are built there, because it presents the greatest need for new housing.

Purchase of land for development in the highly populated areas has run into some difficulties. Private landowners have bought available land for years, on a speculatory basis. Local governments have, in some cases, bought up land, then prepared it for development and sold it to the non-profit community housing at an insignificant gain. In the areas where this has happened, the price of land has stabilised. Some co-operative housing societies and some housing associations that have had enough capital to buy up land to use for building purposes have done so. While such foresight works for the good of prospective tenants, no significant development along these lines can take place until extensive city plans have been worked out. Unfortunately, the potential of the local governments in land acquisition has deteriorated because building and housing funds established by the government for land purchases have not been utilised for lack of actual funds. Simultaneously, the government's demand on the local governments for more self-financing has forced local governments to put a greater portion of their capital into the purchase of land and not all local governments are prepared for that.

Increases in rents for existing housing was part of the housing agreement in 1966. Such increases result when comparable rents increase. Increases from non-profit community housing rents go to the National Building Fund. During the eight years of this agreement, 300,000,000 krona ($40,000,000) will have accumulated in this fund. It will be spent to finance new developments and reduce the rent in the newest projects. Before the establishment of this particular fund, the joint organisation established its own guarantee fund at the beginning of the 1960s when the government severely cut the support of non-profit community housing. This fund guarantees a third mortgage, from 65 per cent to 94 or 97 per cent of the cost, to the extent the government will not guarantee a sufficient number of units. Up to now there was no need for this fund since the building quota for non-profit community housing was increased to 12,000 units and the government will not grant interest guarantees when another fund grants a loan guarantee. The fund still exists and it is a safety precaution for the non-profit community housing.

The non-profit community housing movement in Denmark has for a number of years expanded its field of activity so as to serve all groups of consumers on the housing market. Initially, families with children were given priority, but today, housing is built for every level of the population although families with children still receive the greatest attention. The next priority is both young and older couples, without children. Housing for retired people is spread in non-profit community housing so that older people don't become isolated in special developments. The housing act also permits 4,000 single rooms, with kitchen facilities, toilet and bath, to be included in apartment buildings. These rooms are particularly suitable for students and other young people. They are replacing dormitories in new housing developments since many people do not wish to share kitchen, toilet, and bath facilities with others for a long period of time. A number of co-operative housing societies and housing associations have also lately built many apartments which, with minor changes, become ideal for handicapped people. The higher life expectancy contributes to increasing the number of persons who are older or have a handicap of some sort and the non-profit community housing movement has acknowledged this responsibility. As a matter of practice, however, only a small portion of the 200,000 co-op units are used for 'special' tenants as opposed to general use.

Perhaps a major change in the co-operative building pattern, other than architectural design improvements, has been the larger size of the developments. As the programme has progressed it has been felt that economic and even social advantages can be obtained from size, providing that diversity of tenancy is maintained. These ideas are also employed by the co-operatives, along with the municipalities, in the development of new towns. The co-operative housing programme is working with the central and local governments in the development of projects up to 10,000 units in many areas, in Copenhagen, Elsinore, Roskilde, Odense and Esbjerg to cite a few such instances.

Obviously, it is of great importance that a contractor makes purchases for the construction of an apartment building at the lowest possible prices. To this end, a special purchasing agency for community low-cost housing was considered at the very start of the housing movement. The idea, however, was not applied until 1947. The corporation, Bolind, was established then and it has been the purchasing agency for the co-operative housing society and the social housing associations ever since. The trade unions were the main shareholder until 1967 when the joint organisation acquired the greatest influence by having a majority on the governing board. The corporation can demand the lowest possible prices because of large orders on refrigerators, stoves, laundry machines and on a number of building materials, and this is naturally reflected in the building costs.

This centralisation of the purchases has parallels in the building process. The company Arbejder Bo (Worker's Building) was established in 1941 and has since participated in the building of 60,000 non-profit community homes all over Denmark. The company was started through the co-operation of the Joint Organisation, the labour economic council and several labour unions. Its expert knowledge has been utilised in planning, in the building process and in administration, and in the utilisation of the current housing legislation all over the country. At present, the company is engaged in building several projects of several thousand apartments each.

Several other housing associations have worked along similar lines. The Danish Non-profit Building Association, established in 1942, has built for public social associations throughout the country and has been a leader in the development of several collective housing projects. Several of these projects have won recognition far outside Denmark. The Tenant's Building Association, and other co-operative housing associations and societies, have been active far beyond their base of operations.

One significant reason for the growth in production of housing in Denmark during the most recent years, is the introduction of pre-fabricated housing. This method of building has developed during the last twenty years, slowly in the beginning but now at a rate at of which none of the pioneers had even dreamed. The non-profit housing movement has particularly utilised this method because it reduces construction complexities while not limiting diversity in housing demands. The result, in ten years of experiment, is the standard apartment building with a number of highly developed apartment types. The largest of these apartments has five rooms with an area of 127 square metres and an enclosed porch along the length of the apartment with an area of twenty-seven square metres. There is a well-planned kitchen, with dining area, a refrigerator, a freezer of 700 litres, an electric stove and a dish-washer. There is a bathroom where the washing machine is installed and there is a guest bathroom with both toilet and shower. Furthermore, there are common laundry facilities and other common rooms for a variety of activities. This is one of the highest developed types of apartments in Denmark, built by the Building Corporation, created on 9 March 1968. Shareholders in this company are the joint organisation and a number of its members. In 1970, the corporation started building an equally highly developed atrium house, also prefabricated, which is ideal for family housing.

The years ahead will demand great efforts from the non-profit community housing movement in Denmark. Effective slum clearance of the inner city areas should make sure that years of bad planning—or lack of it—for the low-income families are not repeated in the future. To prepare for this effort, the non-profit community housing movement has established a slum clearance company which, it is hoped, will operate all over the country. The greatest problems are found in Copenhagen but a number of other cities have old and run-down buildings that must give way to development schemes and be replaced by new housing. At least 300,000 out of the existing 1,750,000 housing units in Denmark were built before 1890. At least 50,000 out of these should already have been torn down. A recent estimate shows that one-third of the Danish population lives in substandard housing.* All inhabitants of slum housing belong to

---

* A question of differential standards. See article on Sweden.

4

this group and the children pay the greatest price. That is why the non-profit community housing movement, by involving itself in slum clearance, has taken on the task of solving an enormous community problem, in accordance with the traditions that have been guiding its activities for more than half a century.

Chapter 7 Housing and Planning in Sweden

SVEN F. BENGTSON

One hundred years ago, Sweden was the poorest country in Europe. Today it is one of the most prosperous. Swedish housing is an index to this progress.

Until 1945, housing production in Sweden was greatly restricted. Rents were high, a result of scarcity. The 1945 census indicated that 40 per cent of all units were substandard; that is, housing which was overcrowded, deteriorating, or lacking sanitary facilities. Since then there has been a large rural to urban migration, greatly increased family formation, a decreased mortality rate and full employment, all resulting in a greatly augmented housing demand.

Against this background, in the framework of a generally people-oriented government, the post-war housing policy came into being and a number of policies were formulated. The consistent improvement of housing standards became the main objective of national housing policy. The acute shortage of housing had to be eliminated. Well-planned accommodation of good quality and at a reasonable cost had to be provided for all citizens. The level of amenities was to be raised so that the majority of dwellings could meet the requirements of new buildings in the towns. It was decided the cost of a family dwelling should not exceed 20 per cent of the income of manual workers. In all the areas, the goal was expected to be flexible, influenced by consumer needs, desires and changing styles of life.

Since 1945, Sweden has constructed 1,750,000 units, more than 50 per cent of the housing units in the country. With this construction, overcrowding has dropped from 21 per cent in 1945 to 5 per cent in 1966, or 125,000 units out of a total of 2,875,000 units.

Frederick Fleisher, author of the *New Sweden*, has stated that one out of eight Swedes are not adequately housed, citing the five-year waiting list for apartments as evidence. This is largely because standards of what is adequate have continually increased, making what would be adequate housing conditions elsewhere seem less so in the light of an increased standard of living.

Providing extensive housing necessitated the sharing of responsibility between the national government and the local housing authorities. The main responsibility of the local authority is to construct a large quantity of quality housing and to manage it efficiently. The government's primary role is to provide the necessary guidance, enabling legislation as well as financial guarantees and assistance.

In this provision of housing, speculation and profit were to be strictly limited. Twenty per cent of the units were constructed by co-operative societies, 30 per cent by non-profit firms under municipal control and 13 per cent under direct municipal control. The remaining 37 per cent were built by private builders and over half of these were one-family houses. One of Sweden's major housing problems, overcrowding, had been a result not only of underbuilding, but of the small average size of apartments, less than two bedrooms per unit. (*Using a standard of more than two persons to the room and not counting the kitchen as a room.*) However, only 40 per cent of Swedish families have any children, and only 7 per cent have three or more children. As late as 1960 the stock of housing with two rooms and a kitchen or less was 58 per cent nationally and 61 per cent in urban areas. However, this overcrowding has been greatly reduced since a majority of the new building consists of at least three rooms plus kitchen. At present, families with three or more children have some chance of obtaining an apartment with three bedrooms; and a good balance exists between the number of small families and small apartments. Nevertheless the housing shortage, in the sense of a 'social shortage', is real. People are living in apartments that are too small for their needs or do not have the amenities they wish or are unsatisfactory in some other way. However, many improvements have already been made. By 1960 over 70 per cent of the units had a bath and shower, 81 per cent had a toilet and 96 per cent had running water. The space available in the three rooms, plus kitchen, jumped from 58 square metres to 65 square metres for the two-room flat plus kitchen during the period of 1960–67. In 1966, housing production was 11·4 per 1,000 people, almost 40 per cent more than in 1958 and about the highest rate in Western Europe. By 1966, co-operatives, plus non-profit and public housing, constituted almost two-thirds of all housing in Sweden, whereas from 1920–45, more than seven out of eight housing units were constructed for private profit.

Approaches used in Sweden to provide aid were primarily through the subsidy of the mortgage interest rate and secondarily through subsidies to special groups, such as low-income families, the elderly, families with large numbers of children, students, or special cases. Although the market rate could be 9 per cent, or higher, government guarantees and subsidies brought the effective interest rate down to 6 per cent. Because it was feared that government subsidies plus increasing demands for housing would drive up rentals, part of the government assistance was given in the form of capital subsidy. About 90 per cent of all housing in Sweden receives some government assistance. Generally, first and second mortgages are written for up to 65–70 per cent of the cost. Third mortgages can be obtained in the form of capital grants bringing the total investment or guarantee to 85 per cent for private housing, 95 per cent for co-operative housing, or 100 per cent of the investment for municipal housing.

National housing policy aims to replace about 3 per cent of the total housing stock annually. In the last few years this meant about 80,000–100,000 units per year. The more general housing aims are the elimination of overcrowding, the discontinuance of one-room flats for families, raising of the standards to eliminate substandard accommodation and the reduction of rural-urban differences in housing. An equally important cornerstone of Swedish housing policy is that new housing should be distributed equally throughout all income groups. Moreover, the effort is aimed at eliminating and discouraging social ghettos.

Nevertheless the government takes the position that although housing is important it should not be increased at a greater rate than other segments of the economy such as education, health or industrial development. Hence the relationship of housing production to gross national product has actually dropped from 7·4 per cent to 6 per cent since the 1930s, despite the great increase in total housing and in total production. Similarly, housing as a proportion of total national investment has decreased from 30 per cent in 1930 to 19 per cent in 1966. In short, the government makes every effort to proceed with all due speed, but equally, on many fronts. The reality of Swedish neutrality and the lack of emphasis upon defence expenditure is an enormous boost to the economic potential available to growth in expenditure, for self-development in the field of human welfare.

One of the major factors in housing for the poor and middle-income

families is the level of rents. This is particularly important because 75 per cent of all units are rented, not owned. Starting in
1942, rent controls were instituted and during the war they were
maintained. Gradually, however, the policy changed and today only
25 per cent of all units are under rent control. This is of concern to
social democratic politicians, who believe that most units should be
under rent control. In fact about 90 per cent of the units now under
construction are being built with government assistance and part
of the conditions in accepting government assistance is acceptance
of some degree of rent control. One indication of the degree to which
rents have been kept under control is that the average worker today
pays about the same share of his income for renting a three-room
apartment, plus kitchen, as he did in the 1930s for the renting of a
one-room apartment, plus kitchen. If the tenant is not satisfied with
the rent he is paying, he may demand a review of the rent and a
governmental organisation has been established to handle such
appeals.

Lundberg, one of the leading Swedish economists, suggested that
rent control can be maintained in far more salutary ways than by
imposition of governmental controls. He suggests an expansion of
levels of consumption, by means of subsidies and easy credit to
builders, a classic suggestion by private builders. If the authorities
wish to protect the real income of all families and of special groups
in the population, such as the elderly, students, handicapped and
marginal workers with many children, special subsidies can be given.
One of the major objections to this position is given by the Social
Democratic party who have seen what stratification by special groups
does and do not wish to see the kind of segregated housing that is
so characteristic of many western countries.

A cornerstone of Swedish housing policy is, generally speaking,
that housing shall not be a source of profit-making revenue. Housing
should be built and rented as near to cost as possible; particularly
where government financing is involved. Nevertheless, there has
been a policy to de-control most of the rents except in the big cities
and to exercise control through general subsidies and grants to co-
operatives, municipalities and private builders. In spite of this fact
when Rune Johanson, the Minister of Housing and Labour, attempted to de-control rents on an overall basis several years ago and
made his proposal in Parliament, there was such a phalanx of public
opinion against it that he had to withdraw it for fear of having the

party defeated at the polls. Even when rent controls were relaxed, however, a tenant who was being charged a monopolistic or non-competitive rent still had the right to appeal and to have his rent adjusted; and such appeals are by no means rare. The basic principle is that residential rents cannot be determined on the basis of scarcity. The relationship of rent to costs of production of housing, less government subsidy, is direct. This means that additional demand for housing has to be met by waiting lists. One of Sweden's most pervasive complaints has been that people have had to wait as long as five years for a new apartment, although because of a falling-off of demand this is not true today.

Apart from financing costs, one of the most serious problems in housing is the problem of land costs and land control. In many countries it is through private control of land that public housing, or quasi-public housing such as building by co-operatives, or non-profit housing associations, is most seriously inhibited. Conversely, in other countries it is through the control of speculation by the national government or by the municipality or by the right of acquisition of such land that important advances in building have been made. In no country is this more true than in Sweden. Through land control it is determined where intensive building can take place and what form it is to take. In other countries, the battleground on land questions is whether or not government can or cannot acquire land for which it has no direct use and whether it can control land which it does not acquire. In Sweden this has long since been settled.

In 1967 a major legislative change recognised the great importance of land in the development of the country and gave the government, federal and municipal, the right to acquire land even where there was no immediate use intended. It was recognised that such rights were vital to prevent speculative increases in land prices. Traditionally, development of industries or new towns, even new highways, has increased land values, increases which have belonged to the general population rather than to the individuals who make investments in the right place and at the right time. This 1967 legislation included a number of features. First, the municipal government had the right to buy land when it chose to do so. Secondly, it had the right to buy land whenever it was put up for sale and it had the right to substitute itself for another buyer, if it chose to do so at the going price. This meant that any parcel of land could be bought by the municipal government, if the owner chose to sell it; and all sales had to be officially registered, with the municipal government being given an option to buy within a certain time. This prevented speculators from buying for a possible profit because the municipal government can come in and buy in his place. In order to improve the possibility of local governments making these purchases, the government made large loans to municipalities. It was recognised that there was always the possibility of 'faking' a sale in order to sell to the municipal government but this seems to be a risk which the Swedish government is willing to take.

A major dispute between the political parties of the 'left' and 'right' on the subject of land is on what basis the government should buy. The parties on the left maintain that the price of land should be the original cost or cost price, plus 'a justified interest'. The current attitude of the government is that market price should be a total approach, judged by appraised values of other properties, or what the land will bring in a negotiated arrangement.

Another feature of recent legislation on land is that the government adjusted its tax rates so that land, which was formerly un-taxed if held more than ten years, is now taxed when sold irrespective of the number of years held. On the other hand, owners are not penalised by an increase in the price of the land which results from general inflation. If the prices are up, say 40 per cent from the year of original purchase, the seller can adjust his selling price by 40 per cent in calculating his tax.

Another important measure in the land policy is the land ownership system. When the municipality owns the freehold of a housing plot, it may lease it out to the homeowner against a yearly rent. This Swedish institution, which came into being in 1907, held that citizens who live in or wish to move into a particular area should have the opportunity of obtaining housing within a reasonable price range. The system has been in little use except in the three largest towns. The majority of municipalities have extensive areas of housing which require renewal and with the aim of promoting the land ownership system, it has been decided legislatively to shorten the period for which leases are negotiated—from twenty to ten years. Likewise, changes in compulsory purchases are being made to offer more flexibility to the programme.

In many cases where land owners do not intend to build, their land must be acquired from them, and there is no problem as the municipality builds what it wishes, subject always to the master plan. If, however, a private owner acquires the land and wishes to build something other than what is suggested by the master plan, conflicts do arise, and there have to be compromises. Plans so decided are frequently poorer solutions than if the local authority had had a free hand in planning without having to consider other interests, but they are far better than if there were no brake at all on the private interests.

Long-term planning is the policy in Sweden. Each year the government lays down a framework for the granting of building loans, which is based upon a plan which takes account of all the construction needed. Parliament sanctions the housing plan and provides the financial framework for the current year and for the following two years; the central housing administrator in turn gives to the local authority a preliminary decision on the extent of the loan allotment it can expect during the period and local authorities make their plans based upon this information and can rely on solid financial backing for their housing production.

The local housing authorities provide a five-year building programme, up-dated each year according to a current assessment of demand as well as the availability of building resources. In this way the central government receives information on the plans and achievements of the local authority and grants its subsidies and loans accordingly.

The approach to housing and the necessity for planning for housing is demonstrated in the Swedish approach to new towns. Town planning dates back about a century. Nevertheless, new town planning, in the way it is practised in Sweden, Israel and Soviet Russia, began in earnest in the 1930s and made significant strides after the Second World War. At present the municipal government takes responsibility for the planning for commercial and industrial areas, for schools and transportation, as well as planning for employment and recreation.

Vallingby is a suburb located twelve miles west of Stockholm. Originally, it was planned as a city of 60,000 people. However, it has become a dormitory or satellite city of Stockholm. Business firms were offered incentives to settle in Vallingby and extensive cultural, social and commercial facilities were made available. However, as in the case with many other Swedish suburbs which have approximately 80 per cent of the gainfully occupied residents working in

4*

other sections of an adjoining city Vallingby has not developed as a self-contained city probably because jobs in Stockholm were plentiful and housing scarce. People employed by government agencies or firms moving nearby were granted priority to live in Vallingby and employers felt no great need to move their factories there since the labour supply living there was easily available, even if the firm moved elsewhere. The development of a 'dormitory city' did not please either the promoters or the people who lived there.

Similarly, Skarholmen is a new town south-west of Stockholm. Critics say that it is too 'arty'; that it makes no attempt to consider what the citizens really want; and that there is a glorification of commercialism in that the shopping centre is too huge. The shopping centre, planned to service 300,000 customers was, it is charged, a vision of grandeur. It has been suggested that apartments be built so that walls can be adjusted to the changing needs of tenants, making it possible to enlarge or reduce apartment size. Further, that instead of increasing the amount of equipment and number of amenities, the size of the units be increased. Instead of increasing the size of shopping centres, people should order more by telephone and the goods be delivered either to the home or some central depot of the apartment block. The critics claimed that Skarholmen was a 'planner's dream'. Actually, of course, these criticisms are so sophisticated that they indicate how far ahead in town planning Sweden is of countries like the US where, it has been said, 'town planning starts not with a plan but with a mortgage'.

A 'new town' or new development is the 'company town' of Oxelosund of 15,000 inhabitants, where the Granges Steel Company has its headquarters and employs 6,000 workers, some of whom are from the surrounding area; it reveals the differences between Swedish industrial towns and those elsewhere. The town's council is socialist in nature and only one-third of the councillors work for Granges Steel. The company recognised that it cannot and should not control the city and tries to restrict its activities to providing what the citizens want. To do this it hired a young sociologist who found that what the city wanted most was to retain a small town flavour. For example, 10 per cent of the people own their own homes and more wish to, a characteristic of rural areas though not found frequently in urban Sweden. Granges owns no retail stores, in contrast to many company towns and when it makes investments it does so in schools, recreation centres, or other community operations.

An interesting new town in Finland, similar in character to the Swedish new towns is the garden city of Tapiola. This growing community is not a dormitory town or housing estate but a city of some 16,000, though with a maximum population plan of about 80,000 and a spill-over population already in the neighbourhood of 33,000. Presently there are 4,600 building units in existence and already 3,400 jobs in the area so that 80 per cent of the population will be employed locally. There is a large shopping centre with 65 shops and a social centre. Plans have been completed and building begun on an international tourist hotel with restaurants as well as banqueting and congress halls, a theatre and a concert hall. A library and college of music have been planned, as well as an exhibition hall for fine arts. Tapiola is a working example of the difference between a planned community and a dormitory town. In the planning of Tapiola, high and low buildings have been combined and integrated to create variety and spaciousness, taking the view that blocks of flats and one-family houses, as well as other low buildings, must be placed separately and within their own area.

In Sweden, apart from overall planning for housing, great care is given to housing for the elderly. Although the national government has provided subsidies to municipalities for housing the elderly, originally it was believed that there should be special programmes for the elderly. After a relatively short time it was found that such programmes were inadvisable, both sociologically and economically.

Economically, it was more practical to provide additional subsidies so that elderly families could be housed in ordinary apartment houses, whether old or new. It was far easier to increase the general housing production and to pay a slightly higher subsidy for the aged. Secondly, it was found that elderly people prefer to live among the rest of the population rather than to be segregated. It has been recognised that the changing of location for older people becomes a most traumatic experience. The programme, quite obviously, takes into consideration the feeling and aspirations of the individual and indicates as clearly as any single fact the very advanced state of housing and planning in this country.

Specific financial aids to the elderly include a national retirement pension, a municipal allowance for housing based upon means, supplementary payments for a wife if she is over fifty-five, pensions for widowed mothers without means, municipal help for home services if required, and special aids for rehabilitation of housing when requested. In terms of provisions for the elderly, there is already a galaxy of services provided in the form of education centres, theatrical and musical events, free telephone services, and many other provisions designed to relieve the monotony of life. The emphasis is upon keeping these people in the mainstream of existence and to this end there is much de-emphasis of segregation of the aged, except where it is necessary because of physical or mental incapacity.

In the attempt to limit the rising costs of home building, considerable attention has been given to the development of pre-fabrication or industrialisation of the building industry, resulting in the standardisation of home building through making use of national building standards as pre-conditions for receiving a building loan. The government has been keenly interested in a programme for 10,000 units per year of industrialised building or 10 per cent of the total number built and although originally it was conceived as a two-year programme it has been extended to five years, since it appears that the future of housing is in this direction. It is recognised such approaches cannot work in small projects and it is only employed in projects of 1,000 and more units.

As in Denmark, the method of achieving most of the building has been through co-operatives or non-profit housing corporations. The local authority appoints more than half the members of the board and the rest of the members must be free from connections with any building enterprise. It is, after all, the local authority which is responsible for the provision of housing. The housing corporation provides an instrument through which the local authority can influence the extent and content of new building and establish rent levels and the management of housing. The national government has assumed the responsibility for the handling of loans in house building, the aim of which is to control the wild fluctuations in the amount of building, which were usually aimed at keeping down the capital costs and the rents and to see that as much building as possible is carried out by these non-profit concerns.

The development of housing corporations can be described in a few statistics: of all the dwellings in multiple tenancy in 1965, 21 per cent were owned by non-profit housing corporations and 27 per cent by co-operative tenant associations. In current housing production they play an even greater role.

All in all, it may be said that housing and planning in Sweden is at an extremely advanced level compared to the other Western democracies. Discussions and disputes which take place in Sweden are already far in advance of those which are taking place in other countries; conversely matters which are still hotly contested in other countries have long since been settled in Sweden. It has been decided that housing can only be built in large quantities, if it is financed and controlled by government. Such things as land speculation, segregation of the aged, segregation of the poor and rent fixing are things of the past in Sweden. More pertinent questions are the extent or method of compensation of private landlords for their land, the level of equitable rents, the proportion of national investment which should be devoted to housing as opposed to education, health and roads, the conflict between national, regional and municipal planning, and how much attention can be given to citizens versus planners in determining the exact future of the new towns. These are questions with which western democracies will have to contend once they begin to move into housing activity such as now exists in Sweden.

Chapter 8   Housing Construction in the Soviet Union

YEVGENY SAMODAYEV

The improvement of people's housing conditions is one of the main tasks facing the Soviet government. Thus, the postwar period in the USSR has been characterised both by a large volume of housing construction and by a rapid rehabilitation of war-ravaged cities and towns. During the Second World War hundreds of Soviet cities and towns were either partly or completely destroyed and over 25 million people were rendered homeless. In the past decade, housing construction in the Soviet Union has totalled 1,011 million square metres of living space, or about 23 million flats and, housing to be made available in 1971, in the cities, towns and rural areas, will total 116 million square metres (about two and a half million flats).

Nevertheless, housing construction in the USSR is planned to be increased during the coming five years. In this period, housing with a total floor space of 565 million–575 million square metres is to be built to improve the living conditions of about 60 million people.

For this programme to be successfully fulfilled, it is planned to raise the level of industrialised construction, the degree of pre-fabrication of structural elements and units, ensure a mass application of new effective materials and light-weight structural elements and boost labour productivity in the construction industry by 30–40 per cent.

Housing construction on such a scale has made it possible to offer better housing conditions to about half the population over the past ten years. Every year, between 11 and 12 million people either move into flats in newly-built apartment blocks or add to their floor area in existing houses with improved comforts and in the provision of additional amenities.

However, in spite of this increase in available housing, the population's need for better housing is not yet fully satisfied. Therefore, the local Soviets of Working People's Deputies and their

110

executive bodies register those in need of improved housing conditions and those eligible to receive better housing are placed on a special waiting list.

The order of priority is established by a local Soviet. Top priority is given to Second World War invalids and their families, as well as to families living in houses to be demolished under a reconstruction plan or because of their dilapidated condition, to chronically infirm persons and those whose living space is below the minimum standard. It is envisaged that in 1971–5 the average space per person in new accommodation should be 13–15 square metres.

The amount of dwelling space put into service each year in the 1961–9 period, by state and co-operative organisations, by collective farms and by the builders of private houses, is shown below.

TABLE 1   *Dwelling space made available 1961–69*

Year	Total floor area (In millions sq. m)	Number of flats (In thousands)	People receiving dwelling space, (In millions)		
			Total	In new houses	In existing houses
1961	102,7	2435	11,3	9,0	2,3
1962	100,0	2383	11,2	8,8	2,4
1963	97,6	2322	11,0	8,6	2,4
1964	92,7	2184	10,3	8,1	2,2
1965	97,6	2227	10,8	8,2	2,6
1966	102,1	2291	10,9	8,5	2,4
1967	104,5	2312	11,1	8,6	2,5
1968	102,1	2233	10,8	8,2	2,6
1969	102,5	2250	11,0	—	—

Nevertheless, although the volume of construction is increasing, there is a housing shortage in the USSR. The government is taking important steps to secure a further expansion of the volume of housing construction and to improve services available in the newly-built flats. In order to further such expansion it was recently announced that the goal today is to furnish every family, as soon as possible, with a separate flat of aesthetic design meeting every requirement of hygiene and convenience.

Having all means of production at its disposal, the socialist state is carrying on a housing construction programme on the basis of the planned development of all branches of the national economy, the interests of the people being the guiding consideration. The Soviet Union leads the world in absolute volume of housing construction and ranks high in the rate of increase and the number of flats put into service each year per thousand of the population.

The basic source of finance for housing construction is the centralised state capital investments appropriated under an economic development plan. This accounts for approximately 80 per cent of the total funds. Another source is provided by the non-centralised capital investments out of funds from industrial plants, transport and building organisations. Housing built from these funds is turned over to workers, office employees, engineers and technicians of a particular enterprise.

A third source is from the personal savings of the population, which is invested in house-building co-operatives but which provide only a small share of the total spent on housing construction. House building co-operatives are joined by those willing to improve their living conditions earlier than might otherwise be the case.

Blocks of flats erected by building co-operatives may be of a standard design or specifically designed to fit in with the plans approved by republican, regional, and district authorities. These housing projects are made part of the plan for the state building organisations; the construction period being the same as authorised for the construction of dwellings financed by the state. As to the cost of their construction, the prices and regulations follow lines adhered to in state-financed housing construction. Construction begins after a co-operative has made an initial instalment of 30–50 per cent of the estimated cost of the building. The remaining 50–70 per cent of the estimated cost is covered by a bank credit to be repaid within ten to twenty years in equal yearly payments, with interest of 5 per cent per annum. The volume of co-operative construction is rising steadily and at present accounts for about 6–7 per cent of total housing construction in the country. Utility services for co-operative housing are provided by the state organisations at the same prices charged to state-owned housing and there are fairly large state subsidies for the purpose.

Of no little significance for the improvement of housing conditions is the building of dwellings by the inhabitants of small towns and villages with their own money and with credits offered by the state. Private builders are entitled to a state loan of 700 roubles repayable over a period of seven years. The people living in the areas with severe climatic conditions as well as certain categories of blue- and white-collar workers are entitled to special credit terms—1,000 roubles—repayable over a ten-year period.

Blocks of flats in the cities and in workers' communities, built either by the state building organisations or co-operatives, are capital buildings equipped with plumbing such as central heating, bathrooms, showers, etc. Also, an important achievement of the socialist system is the fact that flats built by the state are available to the people at a very low rent—5 to 6 per cent of the family income.

To maintain existing housing in good condition, to provide for its reconstruction where needed and to raise the level of amenities, large appropriations are made. The cost of repairs and maintenance amounts to approximately 40 per cent of the capital investment in housing construction, excluding the cost of heating, water supply and other utility services. Every year, $1\frac{1}{2}$–2 million of older flats in Soviet towns and villages are connected to the gas-supply network and demolition of dilapidated houses is proceeding now on a fairly large scale. Every year the floor area of houses in this category totals 9–10 million square metres.

In the past decade the building of five-storey blocks of flats has predominated in the USSR but these have been usually built without lifts and are therefore not convenient for the tenants, so recently the building of five-storey blocks has given way to the construction of four-storey and multiple-storey buildings. An expansion of multiple-storey housing construction has been envisaged for the following:

—large cities with a population of 1 million and more, where the costs of engineering facilities, road construction, and public transport are particularly high;

—cities and towns where land for new construction is either very limited or non-existent, or where an expansion of construction boundaries would involve the occupation of valuable agricultural land;

—territories which require costly engineering-geological work for their preparation and equipping;

—urban district reconstruction involving large-scale demolition of old houses.

The four-storey buildings are reserved especially for hot climates and earthquake-risk regions, while the principal types of dwellings in rural areas are 1–2-storey houses constructed from inexpensive local materials, erected on a conveniently located plot of land, with auxiliary structures.

Flats in residential blocks are designed so as to accommodate families of different size. Flat areas are designed, on the average, to provide 14–15 square metres of floor space per inhabitant. But the standard designs for housing are continuously being improved; fresh projects are drawn up to take advantage of new developments as well as requirements.

In contrast to previous years, the newly-designed flats are notable for their larger areas and greater variety, for some of the rooms, in size and layout.

TABLE 2 *Floor Areas of Flats 1961–70*

Number of rooms in flat (not counting the kitchen)	Total floor area of flat		Sq. feet equiv.
	pre-1961 designs sq. meters	1970 designs sq. meters	
1	36	28–38	310–410
2	45	43–50	460–540
3	56	58–63	630–680
4	68	70–74	760–800
5	80	84–91	910–980

The dimensions of separate rooms in flats of standard design are usually as follows:

living rooms	—	16–22 sq. m.
double bedrooms	—	at least 12 sq. m.
single bedrooms	—	not less than 8 sq. m.
kitchens	—	7–9 sq. m.

Some standard designs provide for alternative planning and transformation of separate rooms to allow for possible changes in the composition of the family, for new developments in servicing systems and further advances in plumbing equipment.

Ideally the flats are provided with built-in furniture—cupboards and partitioned wardrobe and shelf-space for clothing, crockery and books, store-rooms and mezzanines for keeping household things, though most flats built up to this time do not contain these amenities. Many of the flats have balconies, and in southern areas, loggias, with floor area differing from flat to flat.

However, it should be admitted that the standards of certain building operations, mostly in finishing work, are sometimes inadequate, although appreciable progress has been made in this field as a whole thanks to the development of the building materials industry and on the basis of advanced technology. In the past few years, this has been largely facilitated by an improvement of the skills of building workers which markedly deteriorated as a result of the Second World War.

The mass-scale housing construction in the USSR is carried out according to standard designs based on a maximum standardisation of structural elements and units. This contributed to a wide introduction of industrial methods, which, in its turn, helped build up a basis for industrialised construction and the change-over to building fully pre-fabricated houses mostly of large panels, so that work on a building site has turned into a mechanised flow-line assembly of houses of large factory-made units. As a result, there are over 300 large-panel house-building factories operating in the USSR.

TABLE 3 *Large-panel building in total volume of State built and co-operative housing construction by per cent in the years 1959–69*

Indices	1959	1961	1963	1965	1967	1969
Newly-built flats in large-panel buildings (in thousands)	16	120	270	425	550	590
Percentage of large-panel building	1·3	9·2	20·2	30·0	32·2	35·8

Large-panel residential buildings under ordinary engineering-geological conditions are 4–16 plus, storeys in height, mostly having carrying panels in transverse walls with either small-pitch (2·7–3·6 metres) or large-pitch (up to 6·3–6·9 metres) setting. Large-panel housing construction in the USSR owes its progress to marked technical-economic advances and to labour requirements declining by one-third in contrast to the building of houses with traditional materials.

The experience in building and using houses built earlier, under standard designs, has shown the need for improvement both in the variety of flats, which is somewhat limited, and the aesthetic standards of architecture. What is more, these designs were marked by a certain monotony of architecture and lay-out, inadequate attention to local natural and climatic conditions, specific national features and traditions of various regions of the country.

Increased attention has been centred on developing new, improved approaches to standard designs for mass-scale housing construction which use a finer architectural style, better lay-out and improved equipment of flats, but standard design practices must take into account the diversity of natural-climatic conditions in the country. The territory of the USSR was divided into four main construction-climatic zones that include every building area from the extreme north to the southernmost borders.

A wide diversity of climatic, geographic, national-domestic and other conditions, all important factors in the planning and design of buildings and interior arrangement of flats, calls for an elaborate nomenclature of housing projects. Beside the main series of designs used for the most commonly encountered building conditions, work is in progress to draw up special structural versions of the series to allow for earthquakes and unusual ground conditions resulting from mine workings, settling ground, permafrost, etc.

All Soviet territory is subdivided into several republican housing development areas. A special series of standard house designs are drawn up for each of them, differing in construction type and wall materials (large panels, box-type room units, etc.). This is dictated by construction material availability, the technical requirements of the building industry, the prospects for its further development, as well as output of the new house-building factories.

Despite the variety of standard design series, the rules of module co-ordination, unification and standardisation of layout and construction elements, in structural units and parts are strictly observed. For this purpose, the State Committee for Civil Construction and Architecture under the USSR State Building Committee published their guide lines concerning industrial structural elements. It covers module standards and the use of ferroconcrete, concrete, wood, asbestos-cement and other materials used in various types of residential and public buildings, with full freedom to vary the form, pattern, texture and colour.

It would be impossible economically to give architectural-artistic features to built-up areas or a specific originality to the city or town image without the use of standardised sections, blocks, and inserts which enable buildings to be erected in different lengths, joined up through arches, for façade, finish, etc. Buildings of special architectural significance are constructed to make use of standardised, factory-made pieces and additional elements produced for particular situations.

To improve the architectural design and lend an individual image to towns and districts, standard house sections and inserts for house linkage are drawn up in blue-print form and local catalogues of pre-fabricated structural elements are then issued. In localities where it is difficult to use ready-made standard designs because of specific house-building conditions (rugged terrain, special compositional importance of a land plot, intricate non-linear contours of houses, etc.) standard sections and inserts for house linkage may be used.

For sites of special importance in a built-up area individual house designs are worked out, employing, as a rule, building materials manufactured according to catalogues of pre-fabricated structural elements by house-building factories of a particular district.

The series of standard designs covers two-, four-, five- and nine-storeyed houses. Taller houses of twelve to sixteen and more storeys are designed within the framework of the series or as experimental or individual projects based on corresponding technical and economic recommendations and houses of nine and more storeys, in addition to long-length designs, may be designed as one-section buildings. Characteristic of housing construction in the past decade has been the more permanent nature of building materials used. In 1958, houses with walls built from stone materials amounted to 77 per cent of the total volume of state housing construction in the country, while, in 1968, the proportion was as high as 93 per cent. About half the total volume of urban housing construction is carried out today with the use of local building materials (brick, natural stone, light-weight concrete blocks, etc.). Recently, however, considerable increases have been achieved in the level of industrialisation in housing construction with the use of precast reinforced-concrete large-size elements (floors, staircases, bath- and toilet-room partitions, etc.). As a result, labour expenses on the construction of brick houses have declined 2·5 to 3·0 times, as compared to the pre-war level.

Volume construction in the coming years will make possible houses notable for their utilisation of radically new designs, designs which are being tested at present, both in construction and actual use. In some areas of the country, houses are being built today from three-dimensional blocks. The new method relies on the workshop manufacture of completely finished block-rooms and even larger parts of a building. As a result, labour expenses in setting up a building are transferred (80–85 per cent) to the workshop level, permitting labour productivity to be considerably increased and construction time to be reduced.

In the southern (particularly seismic) areas progress has been made in constructing dwellings and public buildings from monolithic reinforced concrete in sliding and mobile framework. Using this method the consumption of reinforced steel declines by 25–35 per cent, compared to large-panel construction techniques. This method also entails a reduction in the capital investment which would be necessary to set up production facilities for other systems. What is more, the repeated use of factory-made stock forms and the mechanised positioning of reinforcement frames and mechanical delivery of concrete account for the fact that the building site turns into a kind of industrial enterprise.

Improvement in the architectural standards of prefabricated houses will be facilitated by house-building factories adopting a flexible manufacturing process making possible the production of sets of structural elements for building residential houses of varying length and height, different architectural styles, lay-out and exterior finish and prompt re-adjustment of plant and equipment for manufacturing new elements for new types of houses.

The basic material for supporting structures of prefabricated residential houses is heavy- and light-weight concrete. In addition to light-weight concrete and effective heat-insulating materials for the outer walls, light-weight suspended screen-type walls of effective materials are to be used.

New house designs provide for a considerable improvement in sound insulation of ceilings and walls mostly by the use of special materials and structures, as well as by secure closure of joints between structural elements. The Soviet Union is developing the manufacture of aluminium structural elements, as well as special structural and finishing materials based on polymers and phosphates.

While working out scientific recommendations for the development of housing construction and new standard designs, new building and house designing regulations have also been drawn up. A new, revised edition of the Building Standards and Rules was approved by the USSR Building Committee and circulated on a mass scale in 1971. This document contains recommendations for further improvement of the standards of housing construction. New standard house designs are drawn up in conformity with these recommendations.

As is known, land relations in the USSR are governed by the fact that land is the property of the state. Land is offered free either for unlimited or temporary use to the state, co-operative or public organisations, enterprises and offices, as well as to individuals. In 1968 the USSR Supreme Soviet approved the law based on the Principles of Land Legislation in the USSR and in the Union Republics. It was conceived as a further development of the previously enacted laws, that had established the rights and responsibilities of land users, as well as procedures for the utilisation of land plots, including procedures for building.

Regulations and zoning rules related to construction in the city areas, the upper and lower limits of housing density according to various town-planning factors, including the height of buildings, are set forth in building codes and regulations bearing on the planning and building of cities and towns, as approved by the USSR Gosstroi. All land within the city or town limits is under the control of the city or town Soviet. A complex appraisal of city or town land from the viewpoint of urban construction requirements furnishes a basis for its optimum utilisation in drawing up the town-planning projects.

Technical policies in urban and other construction, under the direction of the USSR Gosstroi, are established by the State Committee for Civil Construction and Architecture, and by the Gosstroi organisations in all the fifteen Union Republics. The problems of urban construction are dealt with on the local level by the regional city and district Soviets.

There is in the USSR a network of All-Union and Union-Republican state research and design institutions dealing with a great many problems such as construction of both housing and public buildings, urban communications and utilities and the theory, history, and prospective problems of Soviet architecture. In addition, some higher educational institutions concern themselves with architectural-construction profiles and are also engaged in research and design activities.

The basic principles in construction planning and design in the Soviet Union were laid down last year by the government's decree on capital construction problems.

The main trends in the Soviet Union's urban construction policy today are as follows:

(1) limitation and regulation of the growth of large cities;
(2) working out a new architectural-planning structure for new cities;
(3) development of small and average cities and towns;
(4) a rational system for distribution of the population, including rural areas, to provide for adequate conditions of work, domestic life and leisure.

There are in the USSR, at present, thirty-three major cities with a population exceeding 500,000, 170 cities with a population of between 100,000 and 500,000 and 1,700 towns with a population under 100,000. Many cities and towns have grown ten to fifteen times since 1926.

Within the period of 1921–69, 934 new cities and towns have come into being in the USSR while the number of urban-type population centres has risen by 2,191. In the post-war period, on the average, as many as 100–125 new cities and towns sprang up in the country, every five years.

New cities in the USSR are built mostly in the sparsely populated areas: in Central Asia and Kazakhstan, and in Siberia and the Far East, which abounds in natural resources and valuable raw materials. These encourage the development of different industries. A case in point is the development of extremely rich natural resources in Siberia. Siberia of today means the gold of Transbaikal area, the diamonds of Mirny and Aikhal, the coal of Kuzbas and Cheremkhov, the ores of Norilsk and Gornaya Shoriya, the hydropower of the great rivers. It also means dozens of new magnificent cities, each with a population of many thousands, such as Norilsk, Angarsk, Bratsk, Taishet, Komsomolsk-on-Amur, Divnogorsk, and many other industrial and cultural centres provided with all modern amenities.

A typical example of a new town is the Academy townlet near Novosibirsk, built in a virgin forest on the picturesque bank of the Ob water reservoir. Its inhabitants enjoy the services of a first-rate trading centre, a community centre, cinema, schools, nurseries and kindergarten, sporting facilities, parks and squares, excellent roads and convenient bus services. Flats are provided with all modern amenities.

A new city, Navoi, has been built within a remarkably short period in the waterless steppe near Bokhara. Where, only recently, there was nothing but sun-scorched sands, today there are attractively arranged multiple-storey buildings with wide pools of water between and a city clothed in green. The Mangyslak peninsula was formerly a wild, desert place, on the Caspian coast. Now it is the site of a new town of Shevchenko, which can compete in beauty, comfort and amenities with any modern city. And many more examples could be given. Also very promising is the planning of new resort towns in different areas of the country, providing medicinal and health treatments.

An important social problem facing the USSR's urban planners is the improvement of utility services in rural population centres so that living conditions in rural areas can be brought as close as possible to those of the town population. This work is under way on a large scale. The main trend in rural construction policies is towards the economically justified enlargement of small villages. Therefore, work is in progress for the concentration of housing construction in the population centres that have good development prospects. Their expansion is proceeding on the basis of specially developed and approved plans.

Local factors cause rural planners particular kinds of problems. As an example, the state farms in the Khabarovsk region (Far East) are rated as having good development prospects and, consequently, are to be built up and further expanded. There is also a need there for the creation of new population centres. Since the end of 1962, work has been progressing on the building of apartment buildings with modern amenities in the countryside. A case in point is an ancient village, Knyaze-Volkonskoe, where until recently there was not a single brick building. In one year, 1963, the village was enlarged by the addition of four eight-flat, six sixteen-flat, and two thirty-flat apartment blocks with modern amenities. A school for 320, two kindergartens to accommodate 140 children, a dining-room with a shop, public baths and a club building with a seating capacity of 300 were constructed.

Quite a few villages built in the Ukraine can serve as examples of good planning, good amenities and outstanding architecture. In the village of Mornitsy, Cherkassk area, an entire street was built within a short time consisting of two-storey houses and large modern buildings serving as a public and trading centre, a club, a dry-goods store, and other public structures. The village has beautiful sculptures and there are tastefully paved streets, avenues and alleys. Green areas abound. The population centres Ksaverovka and Kodaki, in the Kiev region, and many other villages in the Ukraine, are universally known for their style of complex architectural planning.

A magnificent example of new planning is the Platnirovskaya stanitsa (Cossack village) in the Krasnodar area, Russian Federation, which was built on the basis of a general plan. The high incomes of the Kirov collective farmers residing in the stanitsa make it possible to spend as much as 900,000 roubles annually on building construction. Three-storey blocks of flats have been built there provided with all modern services. Also built in the stanitsa, apart from primary schools, have been two eight-year schools, two ten-year schools, seven kindergartens, a hospital with seventy-five beds, several two-storey buildings housing the collective farm's offices, a House of Culture and other buildings. An even more comprehensive building programme is contemplated for the future. It includes, as well as additional housing and schools, rest houses, pioneer camps and a rest zone with a central lake.

High quality is also a feature of the fame enjoyed by rural construction programmes in the Baltic republics. Modern population centres are being built in every district of the Lithuanian Republic. Five of the Lithuanian villages taking part in a national competition received honorary diplomas.

A large number of new towns and urban-type communities are built in the USSR every year around new industrial projects. Most of their residents are building and industrial workers re-settled from other regions; others come from local communities. Re-settlement is carried out exclusively on a voluntary basis through centralised employment of workers for permanent jobs in industry, construction and transportation services by the State Committees for Manpower Reserves under the Councils of Ministers of the Union Republics.

Under the centralised employment programme workers sign up as a rule, for new jobs at industrial plants and building sites located mostly in the northern regions, the Urals, Siberia and the Far East, where manpower for new or expanding industrial plants and building sites is in short supply due to the sparsity of the local population.

The Committees for Manpower Reserves, drawing on the assistance of their local agencies, check up on the availability of accommodation for workers and their families at industrial plants and building projects. There are special regulations enjoining the management of industrial enterprises and building projects to provide workers coming from other regions with jobs and accommodation in well-appointed houses immediately upon arrival. All citizens coming to new towns for permanent work by way of centralised employment schemes have their fare for travel to their new place of residence paid in full and are given lump-sum grants. Experience of many years has shown that 85–90 per cent of residents of new towns settle there for good.

In addition to re-settlement through centralised employment there is another method of encouraging migration to new industrial areas—public appeals to young people. Youth organisations, using various mass media, call on young men and women to volunteer for building new industrial projects and towns. Young volunteers have built the city of Komsomolsk-on-Amur and many other northern and Siberian towns. As a rule, the overwhelming majority of young volunteers accepted permanent jobs and residence in these towns, and care is taken to ensure there are good cultural facilities and living conditions for the workers.

A typical feature of housing construction in the USSR is that it proceeds as a complex with the building of schools, nurseries and kindergartens, public dining-rooms and cafés, shops, medical institutions, clubs, theatres, libraries, sporting and other structures. Urban built-up areas are mostly large collections of buildings that include cultural-domestic buildings as well as housing. Moreover, the services are set up inside the housing estate, mainly in separate buildings, forming part of the overall city system of cultural-domestic and utility services.

The Soviet Union has a network of town-planning research and designing institutes handling problems within their competence on a nationwide scale, as well as in the Union Republics, territories, regions, towns and other populated localities. Among their research subjects are demography, mode of life, per capita housing accommodation, structure and condition of housing and public-service establishments. Research findings are used to draw up recommendations and assignments for standard house designs with the necessary assortment of flats to accommodate families of varied composition with respect to size and structure (sex, age, relationship, etc.). In addition, the series of standard house designs incorporate the required number of types of houses differing in length, number of stories and, in certain cases, in the form of lay-out so as to ensure adequate compositional standards of housing.

Special town-planning research and designing institutes for a particular town or township work out technical and economic recommendations for housing construction in periods ranging from ten to thirty years.

Technical and economic recommendations discussed and endorsed by the local Soviet of Working People's Deputies and building and architectural organisations are used as the basis for drawing up a master plan prescribing the structure, scope and order of priority of housing construction, depending on the size and importance of a particular populated locality or town. Master plans are submitted for a wide discussion to the local Soviets, amended according to their suggestions and recommendations, and endorsed according to accepted procedures.

Thus a new house is built according to a master plan of a detailed housing project. Adaptation of house designs to terrain conditions and selection of the ratio of two-, three-, and four-room flats are carried out by designing organisations in accordance with the demographic composition of a particular region and statistics on population increase and changes in the demographical composition.

On the basis of master plans the planning bodies of the local Soviets draw up programmes for building apartment houses, cultural and public-service establishments. These programmes are made known to the public through permanent commissions under the local Soviets, the Architects' Union, the Scientific and Technical Society and other public organisations. They are discussed in these commissions and organisations, amended on the basis of their suggestions and submitted for endorsement to a session of the local Soviet of Working People's Deputies. Upon their approval they are the principal document for directing construction work.

Chapter 9 Housing in Hungary

TIBOR GASPAR

The Second World War swept over Hungary in 1944 leaving in its wake burnt out villages and cities, ruins and mutilated transport and communication systems. Many municipal services ceased to function and social life in numerous aspects deteriorated. Gradually reconstruction occurred and agricultural and industrial production was revitalised. Housing, however, was not built in any substantial quantity until these basic needs were met.

It was not until 1949 or 1950 that the country could begin to reorganise its housing programme. The country's first five-year plan, lasting from 1955–60, was directed at reconstructing municipal services and basic industry. By 1960, the development of housing and community facilities lagged so far behind that of other sections of the economy that it threatened the successes in other fields as well as social progress generally.

The first five-year plan was a modified success and provided a model for the government's subsequent 1960–75 Housing Plan to build one million apartments. Today, we are still struggling through this plan, having built 600,000 units from 1960–70 (60,000 per year). Four hundred thousand are planned between 1970 and 1975 (80,000 per year). In 1971, 76,000 were completed. In other words, Hungary is now building eight units per 1,000 people compared with six per 1,000 in the 1960s.

Yet, in 1970, the housing shortage was estimated at 360,000 units. This will drop to 160,000 by 1975. However, the prospect of increased population, doubled-up families and inadequate replacement of deteriorating older buildings may require at least one million more apartments between 1975–85. Many changes were made in the allocations of units between Budapest and the smaller cities vis-à-vis the rural areas. Hungary is an agricultural country and for many years after the war more housing was built in rural areas. Gradually, however, the population centre shifted to Budapest, which literally doubled after the war. Therefore, residential building was increased in Budapest and in the projected building programme two-thirds of all units built are located in Budapest and the smaller cities as opposed to one-half the number in the earlier years. However, because of the higher rate of deterioration in Budapest, as well as a higher level of sophistication and effective demand, the need seems even more acute.

The building programme has reduced the overcrowding from 3·2 persons per apartment to 3·08 in the country, a 5 per cent improvement. The average size apartment in the country is now one and a half rooms (not counting the kitchen). There are slightly less than two persons per room; considerably more crowding than is the European standard. With the projected development, up to 1985, it is hoped that average rooms per apartment will rise to two; thereby decreasing the number of persons per room to a level of the European standard.

A major difficulty has been the overwhelming 'one room plus kitchen and bath' character of the housing stock. This has resulted from the one-sidedness of the building programmes of the past twenty years plus the frequent subdivision of larger apartments into smaller ones in order to provide living quarters for more families. The building programme's objective was to provide more individual space and, subsequently, to enlarge the number of rooms and square footage per apartment.

Another measure of adequacy is square metres per apartment. From 1960–65 flats averaged 48 square metres per flat. From 1965–70 it was slightly increased and is presently at about 53 square metres. This is well below the European average but improvement is evident and we are aiming at a mean of 65–70 square metres by 1985. While these figures appear low they are, at least in part, a result of the small number of rooms per individual apartment.

Presently we are operating under standards devised by the Ministry of Building and accepted by the government. These are implemented under our five-year plans and are based upon strategy and plans for housing development. Under these standards, the amount of floor space has been established as shown on the following page. Floor measurements are in accord with the ultimate object of reaching a ratio of one room per person. For the present, therefore, there is slow but continuing progress. Two-room apartments that are currently being constructed, with a floor surface of 53 square metres,

No. of rooms per apartment	No. of persons	Floor space in square metres
1	2	28
1½	3	38
2	4	53
2½	5	60–62
3	6	70

are expected to be occupied by four people. When sufficient units are available, the same apartment will be used for two-member families. A larger apartment, 70 square metres, will serve professional individuals or families having need for larger space.

The allocation of dining space is a recurring question; especially in cases where kitchens are 4–5 square metres and do not provide a suitable area for eating. The trend is towards separate dining areas, even in units with 4–6 square metres, combining dining space with the kitchen or living-room areas. Another solution is to design larger kitchens suitable for dining as well as cooking. The Ministry of Building Standards also encourages allowing space for storage areas, small pantries, built-in wardrobes and foyers. Since there is a public demand for them, apartments occasionally have loggias or balconies.

In any discussion of architecture and building, it must be recognised that aims and means have to be considered simultaneously. Five-year plans have a built-in economic balance which represents the country's possibilities. For the moment, we have to accept the fact that we can only afford a strictly Spartan view when deciding on architectural solutions, lay-outs and equipment and we concentrate on building social housing of an 'acceptable' standard. Questions are considered as to whether it is necessary to restrict ourselves to a 53 square metre floor space in an average apartment, whether living space can be increased before 1980 and whether there can be more architectural freedom in building. Such changes do, of course, affect costs. It is the practice of the government to avoid any building that subsequently has to be torn down and, at the same time, to build on the basis of 'acceptable compromise'. It might be said that we build in the way that we can and in a way that we know, but not necessarily in the way that we desire.

In this connection, it can be said that the quality of Hungarian building judging from the comments of foreign visitors, is quite acceptable. French, Swedish and Russian architects and builders generally comment that Hungarian housing is surprisingly good. I had an opportunity to accompany a large group of Americans through a building site where prefabricated units were under construction and their reaction was extremely encouraging. I have had the same experience with a group of French experts. I have personally inspected a considerable amount of housing in Czechoslovakia, Rumania, USSR and England and it is my impression that the housing in Hungary is of a fair quality.

Through the early 1960s Hungary generally built terrace or block buildings, five storeys and three to four apartments on each floor. They were built without lifts; a type of construction used frequently was a prefabricated slab concrete block system, employing three feet by one foot by nine feet prefabricated blocks.

While there were exceptions to such building, in general state-financed, municipally-constructed public housing was rarely of one- and two-storey buildings. The cost of land, especially in organised, built-up areas, made smaller units even more impractical. Beginning in the 1960s, we began to build higher structures in the more densely built-up industrial areas. First it was seven storeys, then nine; presently, we are building eleven- and seventeen-storey buildings. The use of new structural and technological methods and other lay-out solutions was a great asset. Such improvements would not have been possible without the use of advanced prefabricated methods, without housing factories and without the large-panel systems either in terms of cost or of manpower.

Private housing, which is still an important factor in the country and agricultural areas, prefers one- or two-storey building construction. They are easy to build and require no unusual construction equipment such as cranes, etc. There are no restrictions regarding private ownership in Hungary and anyone may own or build their own home in accordance with their needs or financial capability. Rental dwellings have been nationalised but dwellings of less than six rooms were generally left to private ownership.

Co-operative housing is an extremely important element in Budapest, as well as in the rest of the country. Presently there are 27,800 units operated by co-operatives. Between 1970 and 1975 about one-third of the units built in Budapest will be under co-operative sponsorship.

Housing estates are also built, both as renewal projects as well as

5

where 'new city' centres are developed. An estate of under 1,000 units is considered small with the larger ones reaching as many as 15,000 units. Estates where the occupation density reaches 1,000 persons per hectare (or forty persons per acre) usually occur where the cost of land is high and the availability is low. Such financial considerations also affect the amount of green area, play space per inhabitant, distance between buildings, parking lot areas and even the apartment mix. The recent five-year plan establishes ratios for educational, social and medical facilities in terms of the number of apartments. For every 1,000 apartments built, there must be: ten classrooms for primary school; 100 places in each nursery-kindergarten; fifty places in each day nursery; 180 square metres devoted to public health services/pharmacy; 1,310 square metres of commercial floor area; 350 square metres of repairing services/handicrafts; 150 square metres of cultural facilities/libraries; 200 square metres of maintenance service; 60,000 square metres of playground and green space.

Every five-year plan contains a detailed outline of objectives and appropriate budgets. Responsibility for the objectives lies with local authorities who work out their own plan through the local councils. Councils in larger cities have special entrepreneurial and planning offices (all government owned) to devise plans, to contract building firms, to maintain technical and financial control over building procedures and to turn over the finished building for operation either to the local council or to co-operatives. How the housing investment is handled has much to do with its final success. For example, in Budapest the planning-development office has approximately 18,000 housing units to manage annually. It must keep in touch continuously with the work of various design bureaux and must supervise on-site operations.

The contracting firms, also state owned, employ several thousand workers each. No real competition exists between them, largely because of a continuous shortage in building capacity. Private parties who wish to build a home deal with small, private contractors.

Applications for new apartments are handled by local councils. Applicants are chosen from those who have no dwelling, who live in an overcrowded one, an unsanitary one, or whose circumstances have changed so as to require a different dwelling. A percentage of new housing is allocated to tenants of demolished homes. Partially because of the keen housing shortage, but perhaps for reasons of local stability too, in Budapest residence requirements of from one to five years—sometimes formal, sometimes not—are imposed. Priority is given to larger families.

Each application is placed in one of three categories, depending on the income of the family head. The income levels are set by the municipality. Low-income families pay moderate rentals determined by 'price of use'. Higher-income families in somewhat large apartments assume a percentage of the 'real' cost of the apartment by paying a portion of the amortisation of the long-term loan. The third income category covers families whose income enables them to take part in the housing programme by contributing to a co-operative. The local council is responsible for organising these co-operatives. In both the second and third groups, the families who move in become owners—in one case privately and in the other through a co-operative.

Social committees of the council are obligated to issue annual lists of assignment through the council. Such lists are publicly posted for thirty days. During this period anyone can request a review by the social committee which has the authority to make changes if needed. No family whose application has not been approved can be admitted to an apartment. After occupancy, tenants' rights are protected by tenant committees. Tenants cannot be unfairly evicted.

Rents range between 10 and 20 per cent of family income. For the lower economic levels, family income ranges from 2,000 to 2,500 forints per month; for a higher-income worker this income is, for example, 6,000 forints per month. Rents, therefore, range between 200 and 600 forints, about 10–12 per cent of their income.

During the early 1950s people did not want to move to a new housing estate. The quality of construction of the new buildings was poor, the level of services unsatisfactory and there was a lack of community services. People felt that a better way of life could be found within the old part of the city. All this has changed radically within the last ten years. With improved production of housing, the quality has been greatly improved. Community facilities have also made the estates more attractive. At the same time, conditions in the older parts of the city have deteriorated. Buildings are ageing, traffic has increased and noise and air pollution have become factors that have influenced attitudes. The tendency, particularly among young families, is to move out of the city and into the new estates. As a result of these shifts in living patterns, a new segregation is taking place among professionals, intellectuals and young skilled workers, who tend to move into the housing estates on the peripheries, and the older, poorer, less-skilled workers, who remain in the unrehabilitated areas.

At the same time, there is a corresponding move on the part of rural residents (many of whom work in or on the outskirts of the city) into the general urban area. This is not only true of Budapest but of many central cities of the world. In Budapest alone this change has doubled the population since the Second World War. During the 1950s, to counter this population movement, restrictions were placed on immigration into Budapest. However, this policy places hardship upon many rural residents who are denied a place to live nearer their work and who have to commute long distances each day. This inequity has stirred up controversy as to whether there is, as frequently maintained, not an over-urbanisation but, in fact, an under-emphasis upon urban development. A general approach to decentralisation is to develop 'new towns' around the older towns and simultaneously to encourage rural and urban inhabitants to live in these 'new towns'.

Many critics maintain that these 'new towns' are built at the expense or sacrifice of rehabilitation of the older areas of Budapest and other older settlements. It is, beyond any doubt, considerably more expensive and difficult to reconstruct the older areas than to build new housing estates on the perimeter of the old urban settlements. We estimate, for example, optimistically, that reconstruction is between 30–40 per cent more expensive while the net housing production is not increased by rehabilitation and may even be decreased.

Furthermore, financial limitations of urban renewal in the inner city make it extremely difficult to preserve the areas and to retain their charm. Nevertheless, we should try, as best we can, to devise solutions to preserve this heritage. Such a programme, however, requires a very sophisticated type of architecture and more money than the economy has at the present time.

As a whole, the new housing estates provide acceptable and comfortable living. People do complain about the lack of variety and houses do tend to be alike or similar not only because of architectural problems but for production and economic reasons as well. Housing factories must find ways to produce newer types, in greater numbers, with wider variety in terms of appeal, with new forms, new looks and horizontal as well as vertical changes. While it is hardly accurate to say that the estates look barren and desolate, there is room for improvement in building housing in the future. It must be understood that Hungary, until very recently, has not possessed the means to build estates with the full resources of lively social activities and community facilities, providing the function of a true town centre. The approach has been to build acceptable housing with good transportation, good services and adequate playgrounds and garden areas.

Overall, we believe that the housing we have built is a tremendous step forward, compared to the past, particularly considering the very short period, less than twenty-five years, that the programme has been in operation.

Chapter 10 Public Housing in the United States

J. S. FUERST

Public housing has existed in the United States since 1937, but through the efforts of the real estate lobby, segments of the business community and the press, its growth has been successfully stunted since its inception. Whether public housing will ever develop as a viable programme and rise above the stifling conditions under which it has operated only the future can tell.

From 1937 to 1972 approximately 900,000 federally aided low rent units, plus 100,000 state- and city-aided units, have been completed, or about two out of every hundred in existence. Plans to expand public housing have been continuously made, but little has materialised. Throughout the past twenty-five years individual regions, either through real estate committees, citizens' groups, or local legislative councils, have made concerted and usually successful efforts to block public housing. Despite all the early plans, the programme for public housing has virtually stopped in the last ten years.

During the last three years, an alternative type of public support developed, with public funds being used to subsidise private housing through an interest subsidy by the government. The real subsidy in this programme which induced private investment was a tax concession for depreciation which during an inflationary period allowed large payments to be deferred by the well-to-do taxpayers, hopefully never to be paid. If the units generated by this programme are considered as public housing, despite the fact that they are managed privately under government restrictions, then the public housing programme has increased by almost 50 per cent in the last few years and now comprises about 3 per cent of the total housing units. However, only in the last few years has there been a significant programme of federal subsidy for families of moderate income.

The President's Committee on Urban Housing (1968) reported that the USA needs about 26 million homes within the next decade, about 2·6 million per year at the current rate of population growth.[1]

These figures were corroborated by the report of the National Urban Coalition, *Counterbudget*, which found a need for 700,000 units per year for those who cannot afford private housing.[2] About 30 per cent of all families needing this housing are black and 70 per cent are white. A succession of studies has established that about one-fifth of all families in American cities fall within the poverty class and that about one-third require basic housing which they cannot afford.

Although there is an enormous need for housing among the low- and middle-income families, most of the public housing built in the last seven or eight years has been constructed for the elderly. Most of the 1,500,000 units per year of private permanent housing built has been for middle- and high-income, moderate-size families, in outlying areas of the cities, or for one to four person families of middle- and high-income brackets within the city.

What public housing has been built for families has been located in black areas, while low-income white families living in public housing constructed earlier have, in many instances, moved out and been replaced by blacks. In Chicago, a bell-wether of this change, a 1968 study showed that only four out of every 1,000 white families were living in public housing.

The major problem of the public housing programme has been in racial attitudes. Because black people are heavily concentrated among the lowest income groups and because they form a substantial part of this low-income population and low-rent housing need, the public housing programme would of necessity have included more blacks than a broad general programme. What happened, however, was that because of the attitudes of many people towards living with blacks, as blacks moved in, whites moved out, and the programme took on a black character in many urban areas. Even more significantly, it became a programme directed to the most unfortunate, the most socially disorganised families, with the result that normal upward-striving families, both black and white, avoided it and the better communities rejected it. This attitude towards the programme became so crystallised that all types of rationalisations were adopted in many cities to reject recognition of the existence of the need for public housing.

Private builders are clearly not building for this need. Moreover, the volume of new construction that takes place does not create enough vacancies in standard used units to provide filtering down as a means of improving the conditions of the ill-housed. Units that do become available are frequently in such a poor condition that they must be abandoned both by landlords and tenants, further reducing the supply. A large number of units in many large urban areas, 15,000 in Chicago and 30,000 in New York, are abandoned every year, and more fall into disuse.

The best arguments against extensive dependence on old housing becoming available to lower-income groups came from Anthony Downs in a study done for the National Association of Home Builders and the US Savings and Loan League.[3] Mr Downs lists five important objectives that cannot be achieved by merely utilising the filtering down process.

Expansion of total housing supply so as to keep house prices from rising.

Achievement of some deconcentration of poverty in central cities and some economic integration in new growth areas.

Construction of certain types of units not existing in the inventory but needed by low-income households.

Stimulation of increased activity in the building industry.

Provision of dramatic, large scale upgrading in older, deteriorated areas.

Finally, Downs points out that the filtering down brought about by building of high-priced rental or owner-occupied units ultimately brings far fewer units more slowly to the low-income sector than does direct building for this group.

It has been recognised in the USA that unless private enterprise receives substantial aid from the government it cannot provide decent housing at prices lower-income families can afford. Therefore, although the government has initiated more than thirty special housing programmes for low- and moderate-income families in its short history it has been plagued by stop-and-go financing which has stymied progress.

As initially conceived in 1937, the federal programme was the first urban renewal programme of the nation under which large projects were undertaken to clear substantial slum areas of cities. The initial Housing Act specified that accommodation was to be built of a moderate standard for the housing of low-income families and at minimum costs required to provide this accommodation. The administrators of the programme interpreted this to mean the construction of housing of minimum standards. Consequently, rooms were small; housing originally built under this programme did not contain doors on closets, lids on toilet seats, or installed showers; the regulations compelled authorities to design public housing austerely, simple in appearance and without luxuries for the under-privileged.

The original Housing Act contained a provision that no family would be eligible if its income exceeded five times the rent; in the case of families with three or more dependents, six times the rent. Since rents in public housing in the 1930s were as low as $25 per month, the low rents plus the five-to-one rule resulted in severe restrictions upon the income level of new tenant families. The Federal Housing Agency issued regulations that precluded admission of families whose incomes exceeded $1,400 per year. The Agency also ruled that no family could continue to occupy an apartment if its total income rose more than 30 per cent above the admission limits.

Repeated studies showed that the law and these regulations were causing economic and racial segregation in public housing. On the one hand, many low-income families living in substandard housing conditions were disqualified for public housing; on the other hand, families who were admitted to low-rent apartments were compelled to vacate them when their incomes were still far from sufficient to enable them to obtain housing in the private market, leaving them no alternative but to return to the slums.

An extensive study by the Federal Housing Agency and the National Association of Housing Officials eventually succeeded in documenting the evils sufficiently to re-define eligibility in terms other than by multiples of rent. It was not, however, until 1959, more than twenty years after the programme began, that Congress eliminated the rent income ratio from the law. It was only then that localities achieved some flexibility in determining what families in their communities should be served by the low-rent housing programme, but by that time irreparable damage had been done. Too many authorities had created images of public housing in their community that did not permit them to utilise the increased eligibility limits. In many places even as early as the 1960s the upper-income segment of the eligible families were unwilling to move into public housing, because of the stigma attached to such housing as well as its poor site placement and type of architecture. The really significant aspect of this turn of events was the fact that the USA, as indicated earlier,

5*

has a marked concentration of black families in the lowest income groups, so that by concentrating on the lowest income families the programme was concentrating on the blacks, which made it further unacceptable to low-income whites.

The Housing Act has had at all times a dollar limitation upon construction cost per room built. This dollar limitation remained fixed for years despite changes in the economy and in the level of construction costs in individual localities. The figure, adopted in 1949, of $2,400 for construction cost per room remained virtually unchanged until 1965 despite the pleas of many localities that such cost limits prevented any construction.

Available funds which might have been allocated to a specific region were subject to local option and local determination. Every site selected for a public housing development was required to obtain the approval of the local legislative body. A number of states and a number of localities have laws which require a local referendum before any site can be approved. These requirements for site approval through referendum or through a favourable vote of the local legislative body have thrown the selection of public housing sites into the political arena and have made the expansion of the programme almost impossible. In most localities, the only sites approved for public housing were those where no private developer would build, frequently adjacent to railroad tracks or other undesirable areas. Defenders of this oppressive building programme maintained that slum clearance was necessary and that the new housing should be built close to where the prospective tenants lived so as to minimise 'culture shock'.

Up to the present, the method of subsidising low-rent units has been to allow the local authority to float tax exempt bonds which bear a low rate of interest. The debt service of the bonds, which were usually floated for forty years, was paid by the Federal government in an annual contributions plan. At the outset the regulations specified that the Federal government's contribution cover the amount of the debt service and not the operating costs of the project. All operating expenses had to be defrayed from rents.

Although this system more or less worked from an economic standpoint for the first thirty years, in many localities it was necessary to raise rents to a point where tenants had to pay a higher rent-ratio than they could afford. This also made it more difficult to attract new tenants, who preferred poorer housing to higher rents.

During the last few years the expenses of public housing have risen because of extra maintenance costs and because of inflation, to such an extent that many housing authorities are facing insolvency. Vacancy losses, extra turnover and uncollectable rents have further impaired the financial balance. All these problems have hit the authorities with extra force because of the concentration of lower-income families who, under the Brooke Amendment, pay lower rent and frequently cause higher maintenance costs.

The low construction costs the authorities were forced to obtain, as well as the greatly unbalanced tenancy has, over the course of the years cast disenchantment on public housing. Few have recognised or stated that public housing never was given a chance to succeed from the outset because of the rigid restrictions and antagonistic forces against which it operated. New low-rent housing of the traditional type built from 1962 to 1972 has therefore averaged only 30,000 units per year nationally, a far cry from the 130,000 annual goal projected when the Housing Act of 1949 was passed, and an even further cry from the 700,000 units per year needed according to the National Urban Coalition.

Public housing critics argue that such programmes cannot efficiently or economically meet housing needs, that such concepts are out of step with the desires of the American people and that such housing necessarily breeds social problems. They point to many existing projects such as Pruitt Igoe in St Louis, Cabrini-Green Homes and Robert Taylor Homes in Chicago, or Fort Greene in New York City. They maintain that such projects are not assets. These attitudes would have gratified Herbert U. Nelson, the former president of the National Association of Real Estate Boards, who resisted the 'socialistic incursions' of public housing from the time it was proposed until his death. Nelson, as leader of the real estate, banking and business lobbies, also lead the anti-public housing group in Congress and in the localities.

The attitudes of social workers and others in favour of public housing do not help the situation; they urge that what public housing is available must be provided for the very poorest segment of the community, even to the exclusion of normal, self-supporting families. Fortunately, this attitude is not universal. Monsignor Vincent Cooke, Director of the Catholic Charities of Chicago for many years, has stated that 'public housing, if it is to survive, cannot be the receptacle for the social problems of the social agencies . . . families receiving public assistance and broken families should be admitted but there must be a preponderance of "normal" families residing in public housing to give troubled families someone to look up to'. Coming from the administrator of the largest private family social agency in Chicago, the statement is of great significance.

Of equal significance is an article by Roger Starr, Director of the NYC Citizens' Planning Council, who recants a former social work view. 'I must admit that I used to inveigh against the NYCHA for its reluctance to admit female-headed households into the project unless it had reason to believe that a specific household was relatively stable. My mind was changed by the complaints of the tenants themselves at the way their project was being disfigured by alcoholics, "junkies", and young delinquents, mostly members of Aid to Families with Dependent Children. . . . The devices to be used are simple if we assume that the public housing programme will not be big enough in the calculable future to accommodate *all* the poor families. First the Authority tries to keep out those families whose past records indicate the probability that they will be troublesome to their neighbours and a threat to the physical maintenance of the buildings. Secondly the Authority must refuse to renew the month to month tenancy of unruly and destructive tenants who have, to the satisfaction of the Authority officials, given evidence of an unwillingness or inability to live peaceably with their neighbours.'[4]

Some of the black community's more aggressive leaders insist that their share of public housing be further increased. Black tenancy in public housing in Chicago is already over 90 per cent and it runs over 50 per cent in other cities, so that white tenancy is almost excluded in the low-rent family units. Present court decisions such as those of the Federal Court in Chicago[5] restrict, when they do not prohibit, the building of any further public housing in black areas until three times the number of houses or more are placed in white areas. This may sound reasonable at first in the light of past discrimination but because of community resistance to public housing in its present form, this particular position has further tightened the noose around any new public housing for blacks or whites. As the attorney for the tenants in the Chicago court case said, 'If the choice is between killing public housing and business as usual, let public housing die.'[6]

Even the US Supreme Court validated the objections of some communities to public housing by sanctioning plebiscites as a means of excluding public housing.[7] It is an ironic commentary on community attitudes that the use of plebiscites should mean the kiss of death for public housing, but because of the past performance of public housing this is precisely the effect. And plebiscites cannot be lightly regarded. In a 1968 US Supreme Court decision Justice Black, though standing as a lone dissenter, said, 'It seems unthinkable that we who boast of a government "of the people for the people and by the people" should not be willing to accept the results of the plebiscite'.[8] When in California in 1970 the people voted against public housing Justice Black wrote the majority opinion in the Valtierra case.

What happened in California as well as in Chicago and in the many suburban areas, where attempts were made to introduce public housing, was that suburbanites reacted violently against the only public housing they knew with the poorest, mostly black, most disorganised families being thrust into their neighbourhood as tenants. This reaction has been crucial to public housing.

As Simeon Golar, Chairman of the NYC Housing Authority, described the anti-public housing movement in NYC, the US Civil Rights Division was insisting, in early 1970, that the new national policy was to build low-income housing only in white urban or suburban areas. 'This means in view of obvious political realities that we won't be building any public housing at all'.[9] Piven and Cloward said the Achilles' heel of housing programmes has been 'precisely our insistence that better housing for the black poor be achieved solely by residential desegregation. Reformers must apply what political pressure they have to secure some relief in the ghetto itself'.[10]

In spite of these obstacles, many US communities contain successful public housing projects, with contented tenants and contented neighbours, though not without vigilance. Why and how these projects developed as they did, in spite of the tendency to relegate public housing to the lowest level of consideration, may be a significant index to the public housing programme for the future in the USA.

One good example of that success is the Wise Houses, a 400-unit, twenty-storey project on the upper West Side of Manhattan. The project is part of a 1,300-unit operation grouped administratively under one executive. Wise Houses contains two high-rise buildings, separated by an attractive, imaginatively designed playground. Land coverage is high and it is densely populated as public housing goes, though not for Manhattan. Families average four persons; family income levels are slightly higher than in normal public housing projects, even in NYC, because it is a state and city financed programme and operates a flexible income policy in respect of its tenants. One-third of the apartments are occupied by elderly people and they represent the majority of white residents. The project is an important part of the NYC urban renewal programme and serves families who live in the upper West Side section of Manhattan, many of whom are of Spanish-American extraction and many, particularly the older tenants, are Catholic and Jewish long-time residents of the neighbourhood.

In terms of tenant selection procedures, the Wise Houses project accepts whoever applies. A high degree of intelligence and sensitivity characterises the managers, many of whom have been in the programme for twenty to thirty years. In addition, the higher income limits and limited unit size are plus factors. Wise Houses was the first of five projects to be built in the group and, perhaps, could draw upon a somewhat better level of tenancy than some of the other projects.

In short, the New York City projects, high-rise and conglomerate, derive their success from a population which accepts racial and national minorities more readily than most other cities, and from a housing authority with a staff and commissioners of considerable competence and more enlightened policies than many other big cities.

Nevertheless the New York programme, good as it has been, is not able to operate in a vacuum outside the mainstream of America. Gradually pressure exerted by social agencies and blacks to take in a higher proportion of disadvantaged families took its toll, and New York has begun to experience, as a result of court action, the same problems with housing programmes as the rest of the United States; for instance the recent Forest Hills, Long Island, public housing project against which the suburban population reacted violently. This reaction occurred despite the relatively small number of units, the fact that the unit size was small and the NYCHA guaranteed the nature of the tenancy.

Good projects are also to be found, particularly, in several smaller cities. Valley View Homes of Providence, Rhode Island, is a city-financed low-rise public housing project that has managed to survive and provide housing units and character to the city. The success of this project is attributable to the higher than average income limits, the quality of architecture and the choice of the site. Add to this the fact that fewer families than average receive public assistance, and that there is a good mix of aged, broken, and normal families as well as black and white, and a good picture emerges.

A similarly successful project is Ping Yuan, a medium-rise, seven-storey project in the heart of San Francisco's Chinatown. The project population is almost exclusively Chinese with large but stable self-supporting families. It has a high density, with relatively low-income families; nevertheless there is a long waiting list and few vacancies occur. The upkeep cost of the building is minimal and the approval in the community almost unanimous. The success of the project comes from the attractive architecture, the nature of the tenancy, and the *esprit de corps* of the community.

Kansas City, Missouri, has a 100-unit low-rise project, West Bluff, occupied by a mixed group of Mexican-Americans and a good number of native white and black families. The project is in an outlying area, adequately spread out and attractively designed. The number of children in the project averages more than four per family but since the families, for the most part, have both parents and the density is not great, the project runs smoothly.

A recent book on public housing, *Defensible Space* by Oscar Newman, indicates a good number of public housing projects in the USA which are successful.[11] However, most of these projects are for low- *and* middle-income families, operated under state and city funds, and only a few are federally financed. Newman does, however, mention several good federal public housing projects, notably in NYC and California. These are characterised by a better than ordinary, diversified architecture as well as a better than average tenant group.

Newman indicates that the good projects are characterised by more creative architecture; more entrances; seven to eight storeys and one to three storeys rather than ten or more storeys; fewer spaces not open to view; single loaded corridors versus double loaded ones; and more useable open space where people can congregate.

Many additional good housing projects are often found in small towns. The 1971 Conference issue of the *Journal of Housing*, featured a new programme of 3,500 units in Akron, Ohio where the biggest project is seventy-five units. Much discussion also was devoted to a

Columbus, Ohio programme where the achievement was the de-population of a low-rent family project which had become a spawn-ing ground for delinquency and adult crime and the repopulating and redesigning of this project for the elderly. A third 'notable achievement' is the building of 3,000 units in Indianapolis, which until recently had virtually no public housing. Several other modest successes are cited—a small rehabilitation housing programme in Baltimore and a few scattered site projects in wealthy Westchester County. The document unfortunately tells more of the problems of public housing by its omissions than of its achievements.[12]

Yet this sparsity is not altogether surprising. In April 1965, in *Commentary*, Herbert Gans, a sympathetic critic of public housing, echoed the current belief that public housing is no longer a practical alternative. 'The enthusiasm,' says Gans, 'for public housing has been dwindling and with it badly needed political support. The position of public housing, particularly among liberal intellectuals, has been weakened by the slurs of social and architectural aesthetes who condemn the projects' poor exterior design often in ignorance of the tightly restricted funds.'[13]

Anthony Downs, in discussing the failure of public housing, says that it is not due to the nature of the subsidy but to the adminis-tration of the programme so as partially to make up for the inadequacies of more direct remedies to these problems. This is a euphemistic way of saying that racial attitudes, the concentration of hard-core families and the lack of a firm, positive programme on the part of the administrators have combined to bring public housing to rack and ruin.[14]

Perhaps the bitterest swan-song was that of Simeon Golar, Chair-man of the NYC Housing Authority, in May 1970 at a farewell to Ira Robbins, a fellow commissioner and public housing pioneer. 'Increasingly we see the spectre of having [these things] so many of us have given our lives to, broken. . . . The housing goals first an-nounced in 1937, and reaffirmed in 1949 and 1968, of a decent home and suitable living arrangements for every American family— 26 million homes in a decade. . . . This engine was turned off in November 1968, and we are waiting to blow the train of public housing right off the track. The prospect of building 40,000 units, now in the pipeline in NYC, with 138,000 on the waiting list, is nil. We have a national administration that is paralysing new construc-tion of public housing in the face of a grave housing crisis.'[15]

The present national administration has not only failed to recognise the necessity for such a programme but has treated the Housing and Urban Development Department much as a step-child. Appropriations have been whittled away and interdepartmental questions have usually been resolved with housing receiving short shrift. Moreover the Federal Housing Agency itself has frequently denied or delayed funds to local authorities, particularly for public housing projects.

One of the great oddities (perhaps not so odd in view of the current Federal attitude towards bussing and race) is the way in which race is being utilised by the Federal government to stop all programmes. The Federal Housing Administration, set up ostensibly to carry out non-discriminatory policy, has been scrutinising every programme offered, whether the programme is low-rent housing or the 'new' subsidy programmes, to be certain that all the non-discriminatory safeguards are present. This scrutiny is frequently so thorough as to prevent the housing programme from progressing at all.

Some years ago when it was evident that the public housing programme was slowing down, the Federal government also tried to encourage in a small way legislation aiding housing sponsored by both co-operatives and unions. Nevertheless the co-operative movement which has been operating for many years has so far accounted for only 100,000 units since its inception. Recently there has been some revitalisation of the programme although, so far, there has not been a significant number of units constructed. The Foundation for Co-operative Housing, a national co-operative organisation, has sponsored some 50,000–60,000 units.

Similarly the union housing movement has produced about 100,000 units, mostly in New York City. The United Housing Foundation in New York has an impressive accomplishment in its most recent project of 15,000 apartments in the Bronx, Co-op City. Unless there are significant changes there seems, however, little likelihood of extending this programme into other parts of the country in the near future because unions in the USA are, by and large, not oriented towards building residential housing. True housing co-operatives have also not been able to get off the ground because the bulk of the US population, workers and farmers, have been so oriented towards climbing the free-enterprise ladder that it has precluded any sustained interest in co-operative housing. As an example, in Chicago, where the Amalgamated Clothing Workers recently sponsored a project, only one-third of the units could be allocated to low- or moderate-income families with the remainder going to middle- and higher middle-income families because the union believed that this made a better project and was the only *sound* way of achieving an income spread and enough money to run the project.

In the case of the building trade unions and many of the more powerful unions, the income level of their members is such as to place them well above the median income of the population. As a result their general housing is good, and their interest in good housing for those in the lower-income brackets only eleemosynary rather than directly concerned.

Emphasis has been on programmes such as Operation Break-through, the attempt to introduce prefabricated or systems housing into the USA on a broad scale; subsidies for housing for moderate- and middle-income families; Model Cities, a neighbourhood renewal programme; New Towns; and a number of variants, such as Turn-key, rent supplementation, leasing, and rehabilitation of used units. Altogether the programmes have been very low key.

Operation Breakthrough is designed to help industrial companies develop new building materials and new construction techniques so as to increase the production of quality housing. It was intro-duced in twenty-two areas through different private companies and it appears that real advances may be made in the area of pre-fabrication. The powerful building trade unions, who have been the bitterest enemies of prefabrication, may be ready to make some con-cessions. Nevertheless the programme certainly fell far behind schedule and, as late as 1971, two and a half years after the inception of the experiment, no units had yet been produced.

By far the greatest effort has been channelled into the subsidy programme for moderate-income families. This programme adminis-tered by the Federal Housing Administration, the private enterprise arm of the Department of Housing and Urban Development, has produced more than 500,000 units during the past few years. Subsidies are provided in a somewhat similar fashion to those in Europe.

For example, Section 235 combines insurance and interest pay-ments for owner-occupied homes. FHA insures the loan and pays part of the interest. The payments are in the amount necessary to make up the difference between 20 per cent of the family's monthly income and the required monthly payment under the mortgage for the principal, interest, taxes, and insurance. The assistance payment is available for families having an income, at time of occupancy, of not in excess of 135 per cent of the maximum income limits that are established in the area for occupancy in public housing.

Section 236 offers insurance and interest assistance for rental projects. Here the government pays a maximum of all but 1 per cent of the FHA market interest for as long as forty years. Tenants pay either a basic subsidised rent or 25 per cent of their adjusted income. To be eligible, the family's annual income again cannot exceed a ceiling based on family size or 135 per cent over the public housing eligibility limits in that geographical area, and the family cannot pay more than 35 per cent of its income for rent. Effectively what this means is that the income levels of these projects vary from about $5,000 annually to $8,200 for families of four or five with somewhat less income for smaller families and somewhat higher incomes for larger families.

Non-profit and co-operative sponsors may obtain mortgage loans at up to 100 per cent of the replacement cost of the property. Sponsors hoping to make a profit may obtain mortgage loans up to 90 per cent of replacement cost. A HUD brochure says conservatively: 'Although the cash return to a for-profit sponsor is restricted, favourable depreciation schedules made these developments valuable investments.'[16]

That this is a great understatement is indicated by a 1972 article in the *Chicago Tribune*, which quotes HUD official Norman Watson. 'There is already evidence of a financial crisis in the subsidised housing programme. Investors in the 50 per cent tax bracket are getting a 17·5 per cent return on their equity because they can take a high depreciation expense. . . . Investors never see the property and have little interest in its management as long as they can declare losses against their other taxable income.'[17] In some instances it may be cheaper to get HUD to take over what is a ruined property. In effect the Federal government is providing tax benefits to an owner whose property is contributing to the deterioration of a neighbourhood.

Commenting on this programme, the US Savings and Loan League, in its 1972 Annual Report of Housing in the USA, said, 'These programmes have had many failures because of poor site selection, shoddy construction and inadequate screening of participants. . . . Data collected in 1972 suggest that many federally-assisted units were never completed or occupied.' A news release by the Federal Department of Housing indicated an 8 per cent fore-closure rate at a point when many of the units had scarcely been occupied. Scandals involving overappraisals by 'friendly' FHA appraisers were freely admitted by the administration which threatened to cut off funds to one area after another. In five cities: Detroit, Michigan; Philadelphia, Pennsylvania; Boston, Massachusetts; St Louis, Missouri; and Wilmington, Delaware; 10 per cent of the multi-family units built under the current programme were in default because expenses were too high and vacancy losses also higher than anticipated. Secretary Romney has recently said, 'the issue in the subsidy programme is quality housing because too many shoddy homes are being built'.[18]

One difficulty with this programme is that as the proponents of public housing had warned—when private enterprise becomes involved in a programme, its primary orientation is profit with substantial tax write-offs. Moreover, in Chicago and elsewhere, the owners of these 236 projects have protested the 'unfair' local taxes and have asked for special consideration because of their 'subsidised' status. This request for lower taxes on already subsidised private housing is interesting coming from a group that has castigated public housing because it pays lower property taxes on a formula rather than on a market appraisal basis. The failure of the programme was inevitable as the Federal government has not pursued it with vigour, and in 1973 the new Nixon administration has cancelled it completely for the present, or at least placed an indefinite moratorium on those projects which had not been contracted for.

The Model Cities programme was intended to improve the quality of urban life, at least, it represented a kind of hope for the residents of slum areas. It was calculated to bring citizens of slum areas into the planning process and in a general way to create a multiple-use urban environment with all the facilities needed to live, work and play. It was to be a demonstration programme in 150 areas of the country to make city government more efficient in the delivery of services to the people. The aims were to be met by giving flexibility and resources to a community to carry out locally determined goals. But in city after city the programme has faltered because of a conflict of the goals of the local inhabitants and local administrators. In a number of cases the courts have been called on to adjudicate differences, while Model Cities' funds have been held up by the courts because judges believed city leadership refused to allow meaningful participation by citizens' groups. In many cases citizens have become disenchanted and have not participated. All in all, the programme, which was left over from the Johnson administration, has been a real headache for the Nixon administration and has not had many successes to show for the money spent.

The New Towns Programme has received considerable discussion in the Nixon administration but no significant financial assistance. *Saturday Review* discusses the more important New Towns: the satellite towns of Columbia, Maryland; Foster City, California; Reston, Virginia; and Park Forest, Illinois; the entrepreneurial new towns developed by land fill, drainage of swamps or conversion of large land parcels such as the Irvine Ranch project in California; Clearlake City, Texas; Miami Lakes in Florida or Redwood City in California; the private non-profit Urban Development Corporation in Lysander, New York; the city-in-city Welfare Island in NYC or Franklin Park in Philadelphia; the autonomous city, Lake Havasu, Arizona; the 'Planners' Utopia', Arcosanti, Arizona; and the Federal government's atomic research development in Oak Ridge, Tennessee.[19]

However the *Saturday Review* points out that the future of any substantial number of New Towns in the USA is dim. Anthony Downs, vice president of Chicago's Real Estate Research Corporation, blames the Federal government for its inability or unwillingness to give adequate profit inducements to private builders who see New Towns as too risky and without financial guarantees. Downs said, 'A new town is created if land can be bought cheaply, if its desirability can be enhanced and if it can be sold more expensively.'[20] Significantly, says Downs, even when, as in Columbia, a new town is successful and public housing is invited in, because of foot dragging and bureaucratic road blocks on the part of the Federal government public housing does not materialise significantly. Some token low- and moderate-income housing built by a private non-profit housing corporation is the result but it does not in any way utilise the potentialities of the situation.

Edward Logue, former Director of Planning in Boston, New Haven and NYC, said in the same issue of the *Saturday Review*, 'New towns virtually die at birth in the USA because of the political road blocks'.[31] He cites Lysander, New York, outside Syracuse, where he says, 'the variety of political jurisdictions all vying for their economic advantage have long since carved out of the 2,700 vacant acres their own public service jurisdictions so that, at best, Lysander will be formulated by a series of compromises. The basic problem is that every locality like every developer is trying to feather its own nest'.

As far as alternatives to public low-rent housing programmes are concerned, the Federal government has emphasised programmes such as Turnkey, the purchase of finished housing projects constructed by private contractors for public use. Turnkey was calculated to avoid the complexities of restrictive government specifications which have heretofore raised the ultimate cost of public housing. It is difficult, however, even under such a programme to avoid specifications and standards and, consequently, increased costs. It is for this reason that the programme is so limited in size and it seems clear there is to be no extensive use of this method.

The programme of rent supplements, another weapon in the current federal arsenal to provide better housing for low-income families, offers a cash payment to tenants as the difference between what they have to pay for standard housing and what they can afford. Under this programme cash payments are made to a tenant to supplement the difference between 25 per cent of his income and the basic rental for the unit he occupies. This programme, or its facsimile, was a constant counter-argument against public housing in the 1930s. At that time the opponents of rent supplements objected that it added no housing to the available supply. Arguments in favour of the programme say it will now stimulate the building of new housing and renovation of old by private landlords under specific federal safeguards. The supporters further maintain that in contrast to public housing, this programme is the only way to achieve a mix of families by income and social group. Nevertheless, so much opposition was generated by even this pale substitute for public housing that up to January 1971, only 45,000 units were built under the programme. Clearly, unless radical changes are made in the programme, or congressional attitudes change, this device will be no substitute for public housing.

In an attempt to avoid building new housing much attention, though not many funds, has been given to the rehabilitation of older units. Moneys were made available for improved enforcement of regulations and for rehabilitation loans. Unfortunately there were not too many takers in bad areas because owners sceptical of the future of their area and of their building were often not willing to throw good money after bad. On the other hand, during the past few years, with the growing migration to the suburbs of families seeking to escape what seemed to them the take-over of their area by minority families, vacancies in the cities have increased so that more units than ever before have become available. How many of these units are standard and how far this trend will go, it is too early to say.

Perhaps the most hopeful article on public housing was written by William Ledbetter, Professor of Law at the University of South Carolina, for a symposium on public housing conducted at Duke University Law School in the summer of 1967. Mr Ledbetter said, 'Despite foibles and the many objections, there is no realistic alternative to the "project" in large urban areas where there is an immediate necessity to bulldoze the slums and provide decent housing for thousands of low- and moderate-income families. Land is too scarce, too expensive, to talk of scattered sites in the big metropolitan areas where square footage of soil is as valuable as gold. The problem with design and appearance can be best remedied by increasing the density requirements to a respectable limit.' He concludes by saying that '. . . public housing cannot be replaced by any of the new programmes thus far developed although it can be improved with persistent determination to face the problems and solve them'.[22]

NOTES

1. Report of the President's Commission, *A Decent Home*, US Government Printing Office (1969), p. 39.
2. National Urban Coalition, *Counterbudget* (1971), p. 148.
3. Downs, Anthony, *Federal Housing Subsidies, How are They Working?*, Lexington Books, 1973, pp. 86–8.
4. Starr, Roger, 'Which of the Poor Shall Live in Public Housing?' *The Public Interest* (Spring, 1971), No. 23, pp. 116–23.
5. Gautreaux *v.* Chicago Housing Authority.
6. Silverman, Jane, *Journal of Housing* (June 1972).
7. James, *et al. v.* Valtierra, 402 US 137 (1970).
8. Hunter *v.* Ericson, 393 US 385 (1968).

9. Golar, Simeon, a speech in May 1970 at a farewell dinner to Ira Robbins, another long-time defender of public housing and NYC Housing Commissioner.
10. Piven, Frances and Richard Cloward, 'Desegregating Housing', *New Republic* (16 December 1966).
11. Newman, Oscar, *Defensible Space*, Macmillan (1972).
12. 'Public Housing is Alive and Well and Growing', *Journal of Housing*, National Conference Issue (October 1971).
13. Gans, Herbert, 'The Failure of Urban Renewal', *Commentary* (April 1965).
14. Downs, Anthony, op. cit., pp. 44–5.
15. Golar, op. cit.
16. DHEW Publication No. OS72–15.
17. *Chicago Tribune*, 3 December 1972, p. 43.
18. US Savings and Loan League, *Annual Report of Housing* (1972).
19. 'New Communities, A Symposium', *Saturday Review* (15 May 1971), pp. 20–32.
20. Downs, Anthony, 'Private Investment and Public Weal', *Saturday Review*, (15 May 1971).
21. Logue, Edward, 'Piecing the Political Pie', *Saturday Review*, (15 May 1971).
22. Ledbetter, William, 'Public Housing, A Social Experiment', Law and Contemporary Problems Symposium, Duke University Law School (Summer, 1967).

Chapter 11 Public Housing in Chicago

J. S. FUERST

Chicago more than any other city in the United States exemplifies the promise and despair of public housing. This is true not only because public housing has fallen to such a low estate in Chicago, but also because, until 1953, Chicago possessed a creative programme under which a substantial amount of public housing might have truly revitalised the city. An examination of the programmes, pre-1953 and post-1953, illustrates what public housing can be, what it has become and some of the reasons for the transition.

The *débâcle* of the public housing programme was in part an example of the tragedy of the democratic process. Legislation, such as the 1935 Public Housing Program, fashioned by the conflicts of contending forces, has too often been seriously compromised, with the result that original conceptions have been nullified. Legislation is further impeded through administrative regulations, at the federal or local level, to the point where a programme becomes unacceptable to both sponsors and opponents.

Public housing in the United States began during the depths of the Depression in 1935–6. By 1937, three projects, Jane Addams, Trumbull Park and Julia Lathrop, totalling 2,400 units, were built and rented in Chicago under the Federal Public Works Administration. Significantly, these projects were constructed in white, lower middle-class communities. Mayor Kelly, one of the last big city 'bosses', appointed Elizabeth Wood as Executive Director of the newly created Chicago Housing Authority. During her seventeen-year tenure the Authority made a valiant, though unsuccessful, attempt to produce a solid public housing programme.

Under the programme, housing for the poorest one-third of the population was to be constructed, jobs were to be provided for the unemployed in the building trades and the extensive slums were to be cleared as part of the rebuilding of the city.

The population of Chicago was already among the most racially segregated in the nation and, next to St Louis, had the largest amount of substandard housing, one of the poorest construction records, the lowest vacancy rate and among the highest rent structures, and the highest construction costs. Two of the bitterest enemies of public housing, the National Associations of Real Estate Boards and of Home Builders had their headquarters in the city. In addition Chicago was the possessor of the most entrenched political party organisation in the country.

Despite this the Authority, before 1953, produced numerous programmes and large-scale projects, in an attempt to take advantage of available federal financing. Each proposal and each project had to be fought past the Commissioners, the City Council and the Federal government. Such commissioners as Claude Benjamin, Wayne McMillen, and Robert Taylor frequently supported the fight of the Authority for good building sites. However, the Authority had to run the gauntlet of the city administration and of the City Council, both of which opposed public housing because it was 'socialistic' in general and invariably opposed good housing in good areas because of racial fears. Finally, the Authority had to obtain the approval of the Federal Public Housing Administration which, as sensitive guardian of the 'public purse' and under Congressional scrutiny, frequently created additional hurdles for local authorities.

In spite of all the difficulties, from 1936 to 1953, 11,000 units of public housing were built and 6,000 more were designed for construction. They were as creatively planned as the Federal cost limitations permitted. The first three projects built in Chicago in 1937 were a mixture of two- and three-storey terrace houses, duplexes and flats which still provide adequate living accommodation. Four terrace house projects were built during the war when most cities were not engaged in public housing construction and when aesthetic compromises had to be made because of wartime considerations of money, materials and space. After the war the trend was for two-storey flats and seven-storey buildings. An authority of that period noted that while low buildings were infinitely preferable for families, as land costs and population were increasing it was difficult to confine a massive public housing programme to low-rise projects. Nevertheless, many of the Chicago public housing projects built in 1949 and 1950 were nationally acclaimed for providing economically operated housing which was pleasant to live in and, at the same time, were an asset to the community's appearance. Particular effort was made to keep the buildings from looking institutional. The journal *Progressive Architecture*, in April 1951, gave Loomis Courts, Archer Courts and Prairie Courts architectural awards with the following citation: 'to CHA for startlingly new design of outside balconies, use of color, and use of outside playground space.' An editorial in *Architectural Forum* in 1952, referring to Ogden Gardens and Prairie Courts, stated that 'public housing since the war has done more in Chicago to improve design and planning of apartments at lower rents than all private building in the United States during the same period'.

The Authority at this time was deeply committed to a democratic programme, and made serious attempts to involve citizenry and tenants in planning. As part of this 'program', the Housing Authority solicited criticism on design from community committees, residents of existing public housing projects, as well as residents of surrounding neighbourhoods. The 1950 Annual Report stated: 'If the people of an affected area come to know what is going on and learn how it is going on, change will worry them less. Moreover they can be helpful in working out new housing proposals.'

This democratic approach to housing did not interfere with good business results. A study in the *American City* in 1950 compared operating costs of CHA projects with those of private housing projects in Chicago. Five projects of comparable size, representing terrace houses, three-storey and high-rise buildings were studied. Public housing costs were slightly less than those of the private projects, though the differences were insignificant. At the same time, comparisons were made of the efficiency of operating public housing in Chicago, as compared to other housing authorities in the country. The costs in Chicago, according to an extensive report of National Association of Housing Officials, were better than average for the country. Several studies were also conducted on comparative infant mortality rates, fires, TB-mortality rates and truancy. All of these indices showed considerable improvement under public housing in the late 1940s.

However, it was realised that unless CHA, in conjunction with other city agencies, were to work out an overall plan for the city, to co-ordinate public and private building and to distribute public housing in all sections of the city in order to achieve a sound distribution of families, public housing by itself would lose advances through the surrounding slums.

The CHA monthly bulletin, from 1947 to 1953, regularly referred to the inadequacy of the public housing programme and pointed to the huge unfulfilled needs and the refusal of the city council to allow an effective programme. The day following the passage of the 1949 Federal Housing Act, CHA submitted to Washington, and obtained approval of, a programme of 40,000 housing units to be constructed within six years, of which 21,000 were to be built in the first two years. Each annual report stressed the poor showing of Chicago in relation to other large American cities, in volume of new construction, high construction costs, high proportion of substandard housing, high rents and low amount of public housing. Walter Blucher, the Executive Director of the American Society of Planning Officials, noted in 1952 that 'the failure of the City Council to take advantage of the Federal funds is more than tragic. The need for public housing in Chicago is not only important. It is vital.' After 1940, there was a housing need estimated by CHA to be 140,000 units because of the growing number of people in Chicago, an increase in family size and the progressive deterioration of the housing supply. Yet the Authority was permitted to build housing for less than a fraction of the need. The 1950 CHA *Annual Report* stated: 'This was another year of "slow motion" for the Housing Authority and for Chicago. The Housing Authority has the tools and the know-how. All that is needed is a little of "I will".'

The Housing Authority recognised that the problem of public housing in Chicago was in large measure a problem of race. Slum clearance programmes were inequitable to blacks, for in the absence of new housing that could have been built on vacant land sites, people were simply displaced with no provisions for alternate housing.

The post-war struggle began in the Veteran's Housing Programme in 1946, where Fernwood, Ashburn, Sauganash, and Airport Homes were all scenes of racial incidents. The Authority placed black people in as many projects as it could; eleven out of twenty projects were inter-racial, with 14 per cent of families non-white. The objections of one neighbourhood to blacks was overcome by a court decision. In another one, Airport Homes, antagonism burst into violence, and because of a lack of city administration support, black families could not be retained. In contrast, in some of the other projects—in Sauganash, on the far north-west side, and in Ashburn Homes, on the far south-west side—the atmosphere was more amenable to black people. A sufficient number of tenants were eager to demonstrate their belief that families of all races and creeds could live together and the racial mix in these projects continued until the end of the temporary Veteran's Programme.

In the City-State housing programme, from 1949 to 1950, three or four different and successive packages of sites were offered to the City Council, all of which proposed to use outlying, vacant land. Each package of sites was turned down, for 'good' reasons, most of which added up to 'no blacks please'.

Shortly after the fight for the City-State programme, and during the fight for the Federal programme, Elizabeth Wood characterised the problem in a farewell speech to John Ducey and Milton Shufro:

'The public is cruel to its servants. It creates them and then seeks to corrupt them. The objects they seek are clear. "Just move out those eight negroes." "Fire this man on your staff. He is your only source of trouble." "Don't be so fancy and academic about the sites you pick. Be practical." "The principle is right, you must not try to carry it out now. Wait a little. Cooperate."

'The tragic result is that mediocrity, timidity, and cowardice come to replace what was once our pride, our leadership, our knowledge that we fought for what was needed for the people of our city. Our defeats were defeats at the end of a fight, not defeats from not fighting.

'A federal programme authorizing construction of thousands of homes is coming into reality. This programme has such possibilities that it could change the face of Chicago. But already the forces of timidity are pushing on us from within and from without. What does the city want from this new programme? The fewest houses it can get away with? Placed on scraps of land that officials can think up no other use for? Destined to remain as symbols of planlessness, of political expediency, and of the repudiation of this city's belief in the dignity of all men. This is what you are in danger of getting.

'For Chicago is in a most violent though invisible state of war on the question of race; and every public servant must elect on which side he will enlist, whose enmity he will incur. Though he may seek with all his mind to find the safe way to play it, there is really no safe way.

'In Chicago there are three facts; One, a determination to

sustain a policy of containment by all official acts that blazes out whenever a committee meets on housing. Two, a great overflow of Negroes out of their ghettoes in all parts of the city. Three, because this overflow is against the official will it takes place only with desperation and illegality; and new slums are created daily. The exploiters are having a field day; and the next generation will have to cure this generation's blindness.

'I have been told I am a controversial figure. This is absolutely true, and this is why it is true. I have made every effort to run an honest enterprise. To the best of my knowledge nobody has made any money out of it. We have tried to accept the people as a whole and have tried not to discriminate against anyone unless the action was forced upon us. I have fought for housing, and in doing so I fought with the Federal authorities, the State Legislature, the City Council and anybody else who stood in the way of getting homes built for the people. Of course I am controversial, but so long as I am the Executive Director of the Chicago Housing Authority I shall continue to fight anybody who stands in the way.'

Sites were submitted to the Council for the New Federal Programme, for 21,000 units, to be built during the years 1950–52. Again virtually all were rejected by the City Council. The Authority, for example, wanted to expand the Trumbull Park area and add 500 more units. This was rejected on a legal technicality by a coalition of aldermen and administration officials. The final list of the sites accepted was almost exclusively in the black areas, with one exception at Le Claire Courts, most of the projects were located on slum clearance land.

Integration of the existing Trumbull Park Project was one of the last conflicts for the pre-1953 Authority. It happened by accident when a racially-mixed family moved into one of the first three projects that had been occupied by whites. The family consisted of a white mother, a black father and several children. The mother had applied personally as a tenant and had been accepted. After the family moved in, many families in the neighbourhood, both inside and outside of the project, protested. None the less, the Authority then opened up the project on a truly integrated basis. Later the staff were delighted they had to take the step by force of circumstances, which, to that point, had been denied by the commissioners who did not wish to stir up a 'discordant note'. At first, conditions in Trumbull Park were difficult. Hostilities continued and for several years police protection was required, at considerable cost to the city and to CHA, until blacks and whites could live peacefully together. The police action, the low density, the attractiveness of the architecture and location of the project (the one project where CHA operated, and continues to operate on a 'quota' system) insured the fact that twenty years later there are still 10 per cent black and 90 per cent white families living there.

Le Claire Courts, on the far west side of the city, was the State-City funded project most bitterly protested by the real estate group and property owners of the area. It is the best example of the 'vacant land policy' of the pre-1953 administration and of the passive 'do-nothing' policy of subsequent administrators. This site was obtained by the Housing Authority in 1948 as a concession to the policy of acquiring vacant land sites for inner city residents. It was a 300-unit project built with State-City funds in 1950. A federal project, of similar size, planned in 1950 was built in 1954. This original project was constructed after an agreement between CHA and the Aldermen (*sub rosa*, but fairly widely known) that only 20 per cent of the tenancy would be black. Despite the fact that the black community leadership knew of the pact, it was not opposed. From the outset, CHA tried to get an active development of the vacant land around the project with schools and parks and middle income—hopefully co-operative —housing to create a viable community. A plan was developed with the United Packinghouse Workers Union for a 1,500-unit project, and a shopping centre complex. Unfortunately, that plan was blocked by the neighbourhood itself and the development, apart from the Le Claire project itself, was abandoned.

Nevertheless, Le Claire retained its racial distribution until about 1955. Shortly before this, the housing administration changed. The new administrator was not concerned about a racial balance. When twenty white families moved, the order went out 'fill the vacancies'. No care was taken to see that white families, at least in large part, were replaced by white families in order to retain the originally agreed balance. Instead, twenty black families were moved in. Thirty more white families departed, and again black families moved in. Today, there are virtually only black families in both the original and in the second Le Claire Project.

This occurred, first, in order to avoid rental loss from vacancies.

It was one of the fixed 'rules' in the administration of the housing authority; but, additionally, there was fear of what both the black and white community would say if the units were deliberately held vacant to find the right family balance. The previous administration had taken some pride in low vacancy losses, but this is no great achievement, if the projects are well-placed, well-designed and well-tenanted. Moreover, as previous administrations understood, there were more important values at stake than vacancy losses. Later administrations justified their stand on successive black 'move-ins', even to the point of inundation, but suggesting that any kind of restriction means a quota, a concept which is undemocratic. Secondly, they accepted the principle of first come, first served; thirdly, the huge number of black applicants that had to be accommodated; fourthly, there was a correspondingly low volume of white applicants as the authority became known for operating an exclusively black and poverty-oriented programme.

Le Claire Courts became another 'island' ghetto in the midst of an all-white neighbourhood. As Le Claire Courts changed, so did hopes dwindle for a real breakthrough for public housing on vacant sites and more housing for blacks in other white neighbourhoods. Aldermen, when confronted with the idea of sites in vacant areas, said 'we can't give you any sites in vacant white-occupied areas. You will turn them into black public housing ghettos. Look at Le Claire and Altgeld', and no further vacant sites were given to the Housing Authority. In large part, this is the key to the entire public housing *débâcle* and the forerunner of the 1969 Federal Court decision against the Housing Authority. Passive acceptance of whatever the tenant applicant flow brings can be as discriminatory in its long-term results and is ultimately as objectionable as a virulently anti-black segregationist programme. It was suggested, on numerous occasions, by the Metropolitan Housing Council, the Urban League, the City Club of Chicago, and the American Civil Liberties Union that the Housing Authority adopt a vacant-site policy similar to the original Le Claire plan in order to open up new areas and to erase the policy of 'containment' by an official agency. None the less, the chairman of the CHA board, despite all this organisation support, stated in the *Chicago Daily News* in March 1964:

'What point is there in arguing for or against quotas when such a practice is patently unconstitutional? The CHA is a businesslike operation but we deny that we are soulless. Restrictions of any kind may be hampering at times but it is scarcely up to CHA to question rules laid down for it to follow. We are not a militantly crusading organisation. We have a job to do and we do not believe that it would be in the best interest of the people to force ourselves on a hostile neighbourhood.'

This point of view fairly well characterised the position of the Housing Authority for the period after 1954. From 1955 to the present, a total of some 15,000 housing units were built for low-income families, plus several thousand for the elderly; from 1958 to 1960 about 4,500 units were constructed. Almost all of them were giant high-rises, for large families, stacked one on top of the other in black ghettos. This type of project brought a flood of criticism, but the Authority had little time for evaluation. Between 1962 and 1963 it build about 8,500 more units of the same construction, among which were Robert Taylor Homes—sometimes referred to as the 'seventy million dollar ghetto'—housing 27,000, in which more than three out of every four occupants were children.

In 1964 a series of articles, which ran in the *Chicago Daily News*, discussing the Robert Taylor Homes, made national headlines when it exposed the conditions under which families were living in these supposedly salutary public housing projects. The chairman of the CHA in answer to some of the charges, conceded the existence of many of the problems. He said that in a four-month period, January–April 1964, 'Robert Taylor Homes had one murder, seven rapes, and forty-four burglaries and robberies', but, he maintained, that this was a better performance than could be found in the surrounding area of the project. He conceded that Robert Taylor Homes was 'somewhat unwieldy', but said 'it should not be astounding that so large a group contains *as many different types of people* as one would expect to find in a city of similar size'. The Authority continued to build the same type of structure in other areas.

In 1966, after these institution-like, poverty-oriented structures had received nation-wide attention, the Authority built a new high-rise, of a more original but none the less oppressive variety, also in the black ghetto. In this instance, the Authority, stung by its critics, used an architect known for his flamboyant and interesting but costly designs and produced what was the most costly project up to that point. However, although the architecture was more interesting the

6

tenants were selected on the old basis and the basic problems of the
housing authority showed that even good architecture cannot solve
the basic problems of tenant selection and the existing image of
high-rise public housing.

Why the Chicago Housing Authority persisted in building high-
rises is of course connected with their practice of building in the
ghetto. They made no plans to construct public housing in outlying
areas on the grounds that there was no cheap land available. The
Olcott Blue Book, however, lists large amounts of vacant land, in
various sections of the city, and a 1962 report of the Chicago Plan
Commission acknowledges that many of these areas were in contiguous plots. But the Authority, unwilling and unable to press for projects in these areas, hid behind excuses to continue the policy of
'containment'. Further, the Authority explained, since there were no
outlying sites and the inlying sites were so expensive in terms of slum
clearance, the only procedure for reasonable building within federal
cost limitations was to construct high-rise buildings.

The building of high-rises is not inevitably deleterious as New York
and many cities of Europe have discovered, despite the shudders of
so many social workers. In Chicago, such projects as Ogden Courts,
Prairie Courts, Loomis Courts, to name but three, received national
acclaim. It is true they had less than 200 units and were only middle-
rise, that is seven or eight storeys in height and not part of a massive
complex, yet they possessed much originality in design. Further
experience has confirmed the original acclaim and people have left
these projects at a far lower rate than from the other public housing
sites.

The real problem of the Authority since 1953 has been in tenant
selection which in large part was dictated by its site selection and the
general image of Chicago's public housing. As has been emphasised, the Authority built housing for families strictly in black
areas and it was for this discrimination against blacks in site selection that it was finally enjoined in the Federal Courts in 1968. It
was, however, the Authority's failure to provide for a cross section
of families in the low-income spectrum that distorted the tenancy to
a point that upward striving families, black or white would not move
in and good areas were reluctant to offer sites in their neighbourhoods. Further, the designers ignored the fact that projects built in
black ghettos, reaching high into the sky, accepting the most under-
privileged and socially disadvantaged, often large or broken families

including prostitutes, narcotic addicts and adult criminals, could not operate successfully.

When, in addition, the proportion of children in the population is upward of 70 per cent, because the projects have such a pre-ponderance of large apartments (on the misguided theory that they are benefiting children) the problems become insurmountable.

Three case histories from CHA tenant files indicate families that are not atypical;

(1) A mother and eight children. The father currently serving a three- to five-year sentence in the state penal institution for raping his fourteen year old step-daughter. The victimised girl is at a training school for repeated sexual delinquency and is believed to be pregnant. The mother, semi-literate is alone with seven children over whom she has little control. One of the children is known to have committed unnatural sexual acts on smaller children in the neighbourhood. The children are frequently absent from school. The most recent episode occurred when the mother was found sleeping on the lawn with her 'boyfriend'.

(2) A mother and nine children were deserted by the father. The eldest son was in prison for armed robbery and other offences. The small children are known to have been en-couraged by their mother to steal milk from the neighbours. The mother has a violent temper and creates continuous dis-turbances between herself and the neighbours. The family has constant fights and on at least four occasions the police have had to be called in. The two oldest daughters are unsupervised and associate freely with gangs of boys in the neighbourhood who make the place a 'hang out'.

(3) Family consists of father, mother, and seven children. A syphilitic condition has left the father with physical and mental defects which apparently prevent him from exercising any control over his wife and children. The mother has a 'boyfriend' almost half her age who is possibly the father of her youngest child. For all practical purposes he too lives in the unit. The 'boyfriend' is not much older than the oldest daughter with whom the boyfriend, and the father, have sexual relations. Since the children are alone and unsupervised much of the time they get into considerable trouble. The house is continually

dirty and unkempt in the most elementary sense. The total degeneration of the family has had a bad effect upon the immediate neighbours who feel that their children are in danger both from a sanitary and a moral viewpoint.

These families are not the type on whom social agencies are likely to have a great effect. Living in a housing estate is most likely not of much benefit to them, yet the number of such families who are living in public housing in Chicago has substantially increased in the last fifteen years. The reasons for the increase in poorer families are numerous. Clearance of slums for housing, hospitals, highways, and other improvements, without corresponding building, has left many families homeless. The better-adjusted families have found housing elsewhere. Those unable to adjust, with lower incomes and more social problems, have turned to social agencies, who see better housing as a necessary step in the rehabilitation of these families.

Concurrently, with the increase of poorer family occupancy, the number of 'normal' four or five-person family units, consisting of one wage earner and several children, has decreased. Several years ago a study of slum dwellers indicated that less than half of those eligible in terms of income were interested in moving into public housing which was regarded as second-class housing for second-class citizens. Today the proportion has decreased even more and the majority of these families are black, partly because of the type of families already living there and partly because of the poverty-oriented features of the architecture and the site locations. Yet social agencies generally continue to pressure the Housing Authority, through administrative and court channels, to accept more and more socially inadequate families.

The Chicago Housing Authority since 1953, has never clearly grasped the nature of its dual responsibility. First, in order to maintain a viable authority, the number of problem families housed by the Authority had to be reduced and kept at a manageable level. This meant changing the image of the authority; and it meant reducing the proportions of broken families housed, now at 40 per cent, or of families receiving public assistance, now at 50 per cent. Furthermore, as part of the same programme, it meant building many more units so that a reasonable number of these disadvantaged families could still be absorbed without overwhelming the projects.

Since there would continue to be a significant number of tenant families requiring more services than mere housing, the authority had to recognise the necessity for massive infusion of social and community welfare services.

Much of the social unrest in the 1960s and 1970s is attributable to the dissatisfaction of poor people with society in general. Nevertheless, several tenant surveys conducted by the Welfare Council of Metropolitan Chicago in 1970 indicate that the vandalism in the projects, the lack of concern about public or private property and gang activity directed at other tenants, is directly related to dissatisfaction of tenants with the practices of the Authority.

In the last few years, the specific problems of the Authority rose in ratio to the number of murders, rapes, and robberies, causing many upward striving families to move out. The Authority reacted by asking for a seven million dollar federal grant for 'modernisation' and for more police protection. Secretary of Housing, Romney, touring the projects, said 'police protection is not enough'. But the Authority continued its practice of placing desperately troubled families in the projects to fill vacancies because it could find no other families willing to move in.

In the midst of these practices, public housing in Chicago slowed to a trickle. From 1968 to 1971 only 1,300 family units were scheduled and in 1972 no units were built or occupied. CHA blamed the small number of units on the Federal Courts for restricting the authority in its choice of sites and types of building and then blamed the suburbs for not sharing the burden.

The federal decision which held CHA to be racially discriminatory forbade the CHA practice of building exclusively in black ghettos. For every unit built in a black neighbourhood, the decision read, three units had to be built in white areas. Moreover, the court held that no project of more than thirty or forty units could be built at all. This effectively stopped all public housing. In reacting to the institutional high-rise projects and to the nature of the existing tenancy, characterising CHA projects, the court seemed to assume that housing projects were necessarily the repository of the most socially disadvantaged families. CHA did not disagree with this concept, nor did it appeal for a review of the court order, and also made no attempt to make the projects more acceptable to working-class families and working-class neighbourhoods.

Recently CHA submitted new sites for approval by the Federal Court as ordered to do, however, this submission of 275 sites for

1,700 units (an average of six units per project) was so fragmented that to obtain approval, acquire the property, clear the sites and build the units would take an interminable period, during which period many sites might be eliminated, thus constituting a further delaying action. Most important it made no real attempt to build a significant number of units.

The general policy of the authority has been to react to criticism with token programmes, with bold proposals followed by hasty withdrawals or by proposals tabled after long periods of inaction. These responses are techniques to ward off criticism, to dodge any real action, since the proposals are made without the possibility, the will, or the creative personnel to carry them out.

Essentially the problem of Chicago's public housing is the problem of urban USA. It failed specifically because of the built-in deficiencies of the programme plus the intense racial fears characteristic of so much of the USA. As a result the city serves up many other substitute programmes in minuscule quantities but the housing is built in the suburbs which steadily absorb the middle classes. Simultaneously 15,000 families a year abandon their homes and one deteriorating area after another becomes a no-man's land defaulted to the city. The contiguous areas deteriorate domino-like waiting for some public ground swell to demand action that will revive the city and bring it a meaningful housing programme.

Chapter 12   Public Housing in Puerto Rico

Housing for a Lower Income Segment, a Special Case

CARLOS M. ALVARADO

The year 1940, the New Deal era in the USA, brought new hopes to the Puerto Rican people with the advent of a new administration whose creation was predicated on the dire need for social and economic reform of the island. Puerto Rico is an island commonwealth of the USA with over 2,800,000 people or 800 to the square mile, only one hundred miles in length by thirty-five miles in width.

The initial steps of the new administration were aimed at tackling conditions of extreme poverty that prevailed among the bulk of the population. In order to attract capital from the USA, for social programmes, an industrialisation programme with heavy tax exemption was initiated. The government then began meeting the needs of the poor, especially the necessity for adequate housing.

It was estimated in 1940 that 100,000 new housing units would have to be built to supply the existing need. At that time the US government initiated its low-cost housing programme and the Puerto Rican housing programme was planned to accord with it. This federally-aided public housing programme became the principal tool of the Puerto Rican government in the development of its own housing programme in its four major cities.

For the last three decades the island government has shown great human understanding in its decisions in the area of public welfare and, we believe, that it was the character of the governor and the governing party that shaped this attitude. Confronted with the sensitive problem of tenant reluctance to move into public housing and give up their own homes, however substandard, the government did not force acceptance upon the people. Instead, families were allowed to choose between available public housing or the physical transfer of their houses, wherever possible, to lots which could be rented, bought, or held in usufruct, long term use without ownership. Houses, thus removed were rehabilitated under housing authority norms with financial assistance from the authority. This was the beginning of an urban, self-help, housing programme, which, within limitations, remains one of the best examples of the tenacity of a people seeking to fulfill their needs within their own limits.

A wide variety of housing and urban renewal schemes have been developed and implemented by the governmental housing agencies of this commonwealth. They include: public housing with subsidised rents, both commonwealth- and federally-aided; subsidised commonwealth low-rent single person apartments; low-cost, self-liquidating housing for purchase and core or frame-housing.

There are other schemes including experimental housing, generally with some types of subsidies; moderate cost condominium apartments; mutual-aid and self-help programmes, and other types of co-operatives; lot development programmes, providing minimum services and also lot developments with all the essential services installed; emergency housing that can be dismantled to meet relocation needs due to various types of disasters and moderate-rent housing built under the FHA's Sec. 221 (d) (3) programme. Urban renewal and open land programmes are federally assisted while rehabilitation-on-site programmes and environmental improvements, are Commonwealth-financed. A housing bank is available under which loans are guaranteed for properties and borrowers that do not meet the regular FHA underwriting standards.

There are public housing units for sale and a savings-for-ownership housing plan for public housing tenants. Relocation programmes have been set up for residents of flood areas as well as long-range programme planning, research, promotions and demonstration projects.

One important innovation of Puerto Rican housing has been this self-help programme. Since 1950, the Social Programmes Administration has had the responsibility of developing housing for families living as squatters in the agricultural regions and non-urban zones. Under the SPA programme, about 400 rural communities have been established, providing small parcels of land enjoyed in perpetual usufruct to some 75,000 rural families. A low-cost housing programme has been developed simultaneously, involving the principle of free-labour participation, under which about 35,000 concrete, low-cost houses have been constructed, at a rate of 2,500 units a year.

The system calls for co-operation among neighbours to dig foundations and put up frames and roofs of houses with materials paid for by the government. Although the self-help programme was successful in rural areas, when applied to urban communities it presented basic operational problems, owing to the scarcity of land, with its concomitant high prices, which means the houses are unlikely to be low-cost homes.

Other programmes were implemented to alleviate the housing shortage. For years, Puerto Rico has approached the US government with the proposition that instead of allocating housing units to the island, the US government should be allocating *funds* for housing programmes. The high standards imposed by federal regulations were thought unnecessary, in view of Puerto Rico's serious housing shortage. It has been estimated that with the allocated funds, the local government could double or triple the number of housing units produced each year under a unit programme.

Because the request was not granted, the Commonwealth government allocated its local funds, which were necessarily small compared to the amount available from Washington, to construct a far lower-cost house than was permissible under the ordinary low-rent public housing programme. These low-cost homes were readily accepted, even by moderate-income families, despite the fact that the administration had rejected them because they did not meet the standards required by the US programme.

Slum clearance activities were also reconsidered. The strict federal regulations governing urban renewal were found to be too stringent, causing unneccessary resentment to the families to be relocated, whose displacement disrupted neighbourhood communities and caused ill feeling. This was particularly true in less populated areas. It was decided to concentrate federally-aided urban renewal in larger cities while rehabilitating the slums of the smaller communities with local funding. Most of the slum areas selected for rehabilitation were located in areas where the major problem was the dilapidated state of most of the houses. Families were organised into co-operatives which assumed the responsibility of rehabilitation work under governmental guidance.

The development of core houses, or *casa-techo*, was another programme readily accepted by the people. The administration built the foundations, frames and roofs of houses which were then turned over to low- and moderate-income families who finished them according to their own wishes and financial ability.

In spite of innovatory solutions to the housing problem, the situation continued to be desperate. The movement of families

6*

from rural areas to the larger cities where industries were being established, caused slums to increase in size and living conditions to worsen. At the same time the migration to New York and other large US cities, which had been sponsored by the government, began reversing, as the result of increasingly better conditions in Puerto Rico in contrast to the deteriorating inner-cities on the mainland.

In 1964 Governor Luis Munoz Marin stated in his message to the legislature his position towards public housing.

The fundamental public policies regarding urban housing and renewal efforts were:

1. To facilitate the ideal that each Puerto Rican family should own his own home, if he preferred, in a salutary environment.
2. Low-rent public housing should be considered transitory until such time as a family can improve economically to the point where they can purchase a low-cost house.
3. Blighted areas are to be rehabilitated, when the environmental conditions justify such a possibility, preserving wherever possible the communal spirit usually present in such neighbourhoods.
4. Families displaced by urban renewal should be enabled to select freely, in accordance with their income levels, between a variety of relocation accommodations.
5. The provision of low-cost ownership housing is to be promoted through as wide a means as possible, providing special financing for the construction, reconstruction, expansion or remodelling of various types of modest housing.
6. In locating the governmental housing, justice requires that low- and moderate-income families should have the rights to good residential sites. This urban planning tool should tend to counterbalance the present tendencies of 'social zoning' by promoting a variety of housing types and interaction of economic strata within the new communities created.

The formulation of these policies was the result of a serious effort to re-evaluate the housing and urban renewal programmes. In this re-evaluation, citizen participation was encouraged by civic and political leadership and was supported by professional and industrial groups. Tenant 'grass roots' participation was increasingly encouraged. A dramatic approach to this participation was the programme of *tertulias* prized greatly among the tenants. In these *tertulias*, public housing residents met with administrative officials and discussed openly their attitudes towards public housing. These discussions gave the administration an enormous insight into the needs and problems of the people.

Puerto Rico's housing programme differed from other programmes in the USA because of the much lower income level of the Puerto Rican population. As a result, over the years the public housing projects were not largely devoted to welfare families (as was true in many parts of the USA), but also to low- and middle-income working-class families in Puerto Rico. Indeed, through moving into public housing projects a family actually gained status. This is one of the main reasons for site placement of public housing not being the problem it is in most other areas of the USA.

As a result of a keener awareness of fundamental design values, projects planned since 1960 have attempted to incorporate more suitable urban needs and architectural standards. Underlying the design principles is the fact that the medium high-rise buildings with low land coverage, but high density is a necessity in a densely populated locality such as Puerto Rico. In practice it has meant the acceptance of 300 unit projects scattered throughout the island, low-rise when possible, medium-rise when necessary. These projects have generally avoided the institutional look characteristic of so much US public housing.

This diversity of housing along with an improvement in general environmental character and use of better landscaping, 'street furniture', and unusual plazas and open spaces has resulted in an upgraded concern for the housing facilities themselves. Emphasis has been given to the provision of community open spaces; generous areas of greenery for both active and passive recreation; provision of park areas with seating to promote social conviviality; physical design conducive to the neighbourhood planning concept, separation of pedestrian and vehicular traffic. In all the new projects the concept of the typical plaza has been incorporated to strengthen social interchange and to foster the traditional symbols of identification with the community.

In order to complement the new changes in planning and architecture, a policy of scattering the housing projects throughout the metropolitan urban areas was adopted. The aesthetics of the projects had so improved that they gracefully harmonised with the surrounding areas. This policy, of course, limited the development of huge housing projects, which had been found to be unmanageable. Instead, small estates, averaging 300 units were built but although some larger diversified developments were still constructed very small ones were discouraged because they were economically unfeasible. The use of such urban planning has been helpful in avoiding the creation of ghettos or 'social zoning'.

Recognising the need for a good image to facilitate the integration of families to their new neighbourhoods, a resolution was approved striking the word *public* from the housing projects' names. Prior to the occupation of the estate, intensive orientation work was done with the neighbouring families, to enlist their aid in promoting good will towards the less fortunate who would become their neighbours. As a result of this work, social interaction among families was made easier. However, problems of public housing characteristic of US units, its large concentrations of underprivileged families in large conglomerates were not unknown to Puerto Rico. As an indication of the understanding of the nature of what public housing must be, as early as 1963, Governor Munoz Marin told his legislature . . .

'We are also determined to modify those undesirable conditions prevailing in some of our larger public projects such as Llorens Torres and Nemesio Canales. Our first effort is addressed to revising the design, the space, functionality, and the environmental character of public housing projects such as Llorens Torres, which is nothing else but a city of some 15,000 inhabitants. The plan for this transformation includes providing educational, religious, recreational, and commercial facilities, all of them centred around larger and smaller plazas. It will be necessary to close certain streets and to eliminate certain buildings. A few new buildings with different character, size and design will also be built. The new transformation plan will minimize the institutional character of the project while producing a more heterogeneous community, socially as well as economically. A good economy must produce a good civilization and such changes are, indeed, part of a good civilization.'

Governor Munoz Marin expressed his firm intention to rectify shortcomings in public housing and community facilities; particularly so, with regard to fostering the social and economic integration of the families and the improvement of the environment. The administration had been long aware of this need to improve both physical and social conditions as part of the sheltering function and has continuously worked to this end. Moreover, the government policy is also expressed in the Puerto Rico Planning Board's guides for residential development. These are aimed at both private and public enterprise so that urban land developments comply with a series of basic requirements: population densities; variety in housing types; social integration with minimum stratification; provision of basic community living facilities as a dynamic focus for a healthy citizen life and an aesthetically pleasing architectural environment in accord with the cultural and traditional values and aspirations of the people of Puerto Rico.

To implement the social objectives and government policy, plans were prepared for the social and physical transformation of the two largest and oldest public housing projects of Puerto Rico, Luis Lloren Torres with 2,610 units and Nemesic Canales with 1,200 units. Certain phases of both plans have been in operation and they have already produced substantial improvements in the physical environment as well as in the social development of the families.

The important question is how much has been produced towards the fulfilment of our goal of providing safe and sanitary housing for every Puerto Rican family.

(1) *Subsidised-rental public housing*. Under this heading is included both the Commonwealth, and federally-aided, conventionally developed, housing for rent; the Commonwealth low-rent, single person apartments; and the federally-aided turnkey public housing programme. Table 1 shows the total dwelling units constructed were 51,000 with 5,000 under construction and 11,000 in planning.

(2) *Commonwealth Housing Programme*. Under this heading are included the core or frame house, the moderate-cost condominium experimental housing for sale, lot development subdivisions (which greatly facilitate and promote the social objective of home ownership for low-income families), co-operative and the self-liquidating low-cost housing programmes. This programme has produced about half as many units. The governmental assistance in these ownership-oriented housing programmes has provided living quarters for over 250,000 persons unable to afford the market price of standard housing, at an average cost of about $8,000 per unit, around half the price of conventional public housing.

TABLE 1. *Public rental housing in Puerto Rico as of 30 June 1973, by number of units managed, in construction, and number of units in planning and by expenditures, and in whole or in part subsidized by US Federal funds.*

By stage of unit	Number of units	Amount of expenditure in millions of dollars†	Average cost per unit $
Completed	50,983	523	10,256
In Construction	5,118	90	17,663*
In Planning	10,825	197	18,198*
Totals	66,926	810	‡

* Estimated expenditures.
† Figures rounded to nearest million.
‡ Not applicable.

TABLE 2. *Low cost housing produced for sale to private families in Puerto Rico as of 30 June 1973, under the Commonwealth low cost housing program.*

By stage of unit	Number of units	Amount of expenditure in millions of dollars†	average cost per unit $
Completed	14,741	124	8,280
Under Construction	5,624	‡	‡
In Planning	17,192	‡	‡
Totals	37,557	462	‡

† Figures rounded to nearest million.
‡ Not applicable.
Source: Puerto Rico Dept. CRUU

Today the urban slum index is less than half of what it was three decades ago: from 80 per cent in 1940 to about 70 per cent in 1950, to 41 per cent in 1960, and nearing 30 per cent by 1969. About 80 per cent of the 25,000 households displaced from blighted and slum areas through urban renewal have been relocated in better areas and this has increased the range of housing choice among the very poor.

There has been a marked increase in the volume and variety of governmental housing. During the 1940s, eighty out of a hundred government-sponsored dwellings were subsidised. Although conventional public housing pushed ahead sharply, other programmes were also introduced such as the self-help programme, and the lower-cost public housing low-rental apartments. Today, among Puerto Rican families applying for assistance from the government for urban housing, 50 per cent will be located in a conventional subsidised low-rental project and 50 per cent will choose from other alternatives, with many moving into areas of single family dwelling where home owners constitute an organisational backbone for the neighbourhood. Actually while home ownership is, as indicated by Munoz Marin, a goal, current needs mean that rental projects will be with us for a long time to come.

The PR Housing Authority has also recognised the need to produce housing solutions that meet the specific requirements of our metropolitan circumstances and that are in keeping with the strong demand for improved architectural design and town planning. The concept of apartments in multi-storey residential complexes has been successfully promoted for the San Juan Metropolitan Area, and of course to some extent negates the possibility of small projects. Similarly the extensive use of these large complexes does add to the stock of rented accommodation rather than developing the concept of home ownership.

This approach has produced the El Monte project, which received the FHA and URA awards and has been praised in prestigious architectural journals of international circulation. The Quintana Complex, containing subsidised public housing, low-rise moderate-rental apartments, and high-rise condominium dwellings, is another fine example of the integration of housing of diverse types and wise utilisation of Puerto Rico's scarce land resources. The Berwind and Cupey developments have used integrated communities of multiple housing types for families of all economic levels where the visual monotony will be at a minimum and where good urban design practices have been incorporated. Two years ago, the magazine *Progressive Architecture* awarded a first prize to the ingenious public housing solution proposed for the La Puntilla sector, in the Old San Juan islet.

In general while population growth continues at an accelerated pace with the total population estimated at 6,000,000 by the year 2000, and while much of the population is concentrated in urban areas, there is an urgent need for urban development policy to guide future settlement of population growth. The present policy of locating industries in urban areas should be re-examined and priority given to channelling industry to smaller towns. Likewise, this alarming population density requires the most careful use of its acres of flat land for housing; low-density single family units should be discouraged. This has important implications for rented accommodation and home ownership in the future as well as for industrialised housing.

Two important innovations illustrate Puerto Rico's search for practical low-cost housing. The first is the self-help and mutual aid programme for the very poor family. Although this system is best suited to the rural programmes, the urban counterpart, using the core houses, the home-site development and the on-site rehabilitation scheme, have provided some practical answers to the re-housing of the lowest income groups. As indicated above, this type of response may well be short term rather than long term in terms of providing ultimate solutions. The second innovation is the development of new construction techniques designed to produce significant cost reductions. The Housing Administration has directly experimented with prefabrication components, has promoted an interest in prefabrication among dozens of private housing developers, and at present, is buying thousands of prefabricated houses for a self-liquidating low-cost programme. This governmental encouragement and growing use of prefabricated components tends to eliminate the uncertainties of the market and has introduced new housing practices into a rather conservative society.

Puerto Rico has recognised that their high density housing with generous open space areas can only succeed by introducing industrialised construction processes. This will increase production of housing and will substantially reduce its price. In the past, CRUV (Puerto Rican Housing Authority) has encouraged private industry to go into research activities for the production of industrialised housing. This research has enabled seven of our local construction firms to submit proposals to the Operation Breakthrough Programme now being sponsored by the Federal Housing and Urban Affairs

Department. One of these industrialised systems—the Shelley System—is now in use for the construction of public housing in Puerto Rico. Admittedly, one of the factors that makes pre-fabrication and industrialised housing feasible in Puerto Rico is the existence of large masses of under-housed families in a relatively small area. In the first place the geographical proximity is most suitable for factory produced housing; and in the second, people's expectations are not quite as high as on the mainland.

Another important innovation of which Puerto Rico is most proud and which may well hold the key to the future, is the policy on land. In 1964 a Land Administration was created by law. In effect it was a Land Bank. This Administration has been active in the advanced acquisition of large tracts of land in order to cope with the further inflation of land values. This land may be made available to house builders—both public and private—even at a price below cost. The Administration has also been active in the rehabilitation and recovery of unused public lands. A programme for buying of land similar to one successfully used in Scandinavia has been introduced in Puerto Rico. Under it local public agencies can buy land, without necessarily building on it immediately. The work done by the Administration is beginning to pay dividends. Through this effort, land values have been kept at reasonable levels and land has been made available for the development of intensive industrialised housing programmes.

We are convinced that this governmental work has enhanced the metropolitan urban scene by a more rational utilisation of the land, by its architectural value, by its functional integration with the natural contours and existing vegetation of certain sites, by its democratic philosophy of socio-economic integration and its emphasis on the incorporation of the best elements of urban design.

Chapter 13 Conclusions

J. S. FUERST

Public housing has made available low-cost living accommodations to large groups of people throughout the world. In many countries it accounts for a large proportion of all housing and in many others, where governmental housing has been less developed, alternative methods of non-profit housing have been successfully employed for meeting the needs of low- and moderate-income families.

About 35 per cent of all housing in Great Britain is under governmental auspices. In West Germany and Denmark 33 per cent of all housing units are either under co-operative, union or public auspices. In France, the public housing figure is about 15 per cent of housing stock plus one-third of current production. In Israel over 50 per cent of all housing is either operated by the government, by co-operatives or by unions. In the Soviet Union, all mass housing has been built under governmental auspices. Clearly, non-private housing is a significant part of the picture in the advanced Western countries.

An important feature distinguishing one programme from another is the approach to tenant selection. Rents, administrative techniques and personal preferences have caused broad stratification of families in English, French and Danish public-aided housing. However, this has not always been the case. Forty years ago, when the governments of France, England and Denmark first began government housing programmes, similar to those in the USA, they, too, reached for the lowest-income families. Fears existed that government housing would encroach upon private interests. But private interests were not powerful enough in these countries to force the governments to serve only low-income families, as happened in the United States. Perhaps more important, there was a broad public demand for this housing and the electorate would not allow it to go in the direction of welfare families exclusively. In fact, in Britain and France some argue— frequently those lukewarm on public housing—that public housing is not made available sufficiently to the lowest-income groups.

178

On the other hand, the Ministry of Housing in Denmark is directing its efforts to avoid the creation of modern slum neighbourhoods, by urging housing societies, the quasi-public building arm, 'to mix categories of housing which are comparable in technical standards. The trend towards integration of various income groups is evident in the latest legislation.'[1] In England, such attempts have also been made. The 1967 annual report of the Greater London Council, referring to a particular local municipal housing project in a marginal neighbourhood, stated, 'There is need for more variety in the social structure in the larger new housing developments so as to avoid social imbalance. . . . There is need to redress this imbalance in areas where it presently exists.' Although poorer families do live in government supported housing in Britain, attempts are made to prevent such housing from becoming economic ghettos.

More recently the Conservative government's policy has attempted to favour the lower-income family somewhat more than the previous policy. Although single persons and older families have only been accepted as tenants in limited numbers, no one has been excluded, and a good social mix has been maintained. As a result, few, if any, consider public housing as 'second-class citizenship'.

Similarly, in France, the projects for low- and moderate-income families are mixed, and legislation in the last few years has increased the mixing even more. Furthermore, placing developments close to private homes has not presented serious community problems. Land prices, however, frequently are so high as to preclude the placing of the public projects in high value areas because of cost limitations.

In Israel, conscious efforts are made to mix economic as well as differing national groups but such efforts have not always worked. A Gresham's Law tends to exist, with the presence of large groups of lower socio-economic families causing higher level families to move. The government is aware of this problem and has taken some steps to counteract it. One approach has been to house certain national groups in certain locations, providing them with the opportunity to mix with other groups at schools, employment situations, shopping plazas, churches, hospitals and recreational centres. It is generally agreed that where public housing has been successful careful tenant selection was indispensable. A variant of this mixing problem exists in the USA, where tenant selection for a small number of vacancies is determined by a long waiting list, fairly inflexible priorities and misguided social agency pressures, which often polarise the tenancy into the lowest income group.

The problem of integrating low-income families with middle-income families is made more complex when the tenants are the lowest of the low-income families. Where the circumstances are compounded by serious social problems, such as alcoholism, prostitution, feeble-mindedness, marital discord, acts of anti-social behaviour and narcotic addiction, the solution is much more difficult to achieve. Often, the supporters of public housing feel guilty about rejecting any needy family and thus the average falls to the level of the lowest economic type.

Occasionally, however, conscious stratification of groups has been attempted, as in the 'half-way houses' of London or the projects for 'socially unbalanced families' in Holland. In England local borough welfare departments have for years maintained a stock of older, usually reconditioned, flats known as 'half-way houses' in which evicted families, or those unable to manage in private housing, are placed on a temporary basis. An ingenious experiment in handling such families was tried by Holland during a period of forty years. The families were first located in segregated 'camps' where they were given intensive social service assistance, in providing employment, schooling, homemaker service and other needs. Simultaneously, Holland established six housing projects, containing a maximum of 200 units each, in which only families with serious social problems were located. Experience proved that without heavy reliance on social services, both project conditions and occupants' attitudes deteriorated rapidly. Where social services were available, projects remained adequate in physical facilities and some families showed improvement. The projects ranged from providing massive social services to those that contained no such services at all. The government eventually concluded that such projects segregated occupants too sharply from the community and the costs were greater than the advantages obtained. Presently, the government does not build such projects but instead builds moderately large public housing projects and includes a controlled percentage of families with serious problems. In contact with functioning families, plus outside services, these families improve their social situation somewhat more effectively.

It is important, though sometimes difficult, to differentiate between the socially unbalanced families and those families who find it difficult to adjust to living in housing projects for cultural rather than individual reasons. Gypsies and some Arabs in France, rural blacks from the south in the USA, or Moroccan and Libyan Jews in Israel and many southern European immigrants in Sweden or Switzerland present examples of the latter. Certainly there is some overlap in both groups but the different methods of handling them are the key to success. A French study indicated that 10 per cent culturally alienated families is about the highest proportion which can easily be absorbed, 15–20 per cent when the differences are less.[2]

A project seemingly can absorb only 2–3 per cent of the socially unbalanced before the project becomes unacceptable to low- and middle-income families striving for upward mobility. Holland, moreover, recognised that socially unbalanced families can be divided into those who can benefit from treatment and services, and those who cannot. Furthermore, Holland learned that placing a large number of such families in the projects does nothing for such families and lowers the living standard for the remainder of the project inhabitants.

A great problem is how to handle hard-core families once they are in the projects in substantial number. As M. W. Newman said in the Chicago *Daily News*, 'Courts and government rulings are making it harder to evict problem families'. With this sort of thing in mind Manny Hildes, manager of the Stephen Wise project in NYC, confided to Newman, 'It's quite hard to get anyone out now so the big hope is not to let that kind of family get in'. Newman says that while this talk may rub some people the wrong way, practical people who want to make public housing work often talk like Hildes.[3]

Two experiments are particularly significant in this regard. In Puerto Rico, Nemesio Canales was the subject of an intensive federal-local study. This project had been the 'dumping ground' for the most underprivileged families from the two worst slums in Puerto Rico, 'La Perla' and 'Martin Pena'. Nemesio Canales had all the problems that characterise Robert Taylor, a Chicago project, and Pruitt Igoe of St Louis. The administration, local and federal, decided that the undesirable conditions in the project had to be remedied and took the following steps:

Weed out as painlessly as possible the hard core delinquents and anti-social families who were not able to adjust to project living and who made it difficult for others. These tenants were to be relocated elsewhere in half-way houses, rehabilitated older houses, until they can better adjust. Reduce the density of projects by not filling vacancies or filling them with small, self-supporting families, all of whom had a mother, father and some children.

Convert vacant units to community facilities such as infant welfare stations, libraries, craft centres, drama rooms, extra classrooms and study rooms.

Health, educational, recreational, vocational services and agencies as well as more commercial (preferably co-operative) facilities were brought in.

Convert some of the smaller vacant units, if necessary, to handle the larger families who remained on the project.

Also when the project was de-densified some of the larger units would be converted to smaller units.[4]

These specific alterations plus many more are making both Nemesio Canales and Llorens Torres more manageable and more livable projects for the families who remain and the neighbours who surround them.

Successful projects are apparently largely a matter of building public projects that are no different in concept to private ones and controlling the tenancy. Neither integration nor segregation, nor concentration of large or small families, is the *summum bonum* in effective housing project operation. Neither high-rise nor low-rise buildings are the sole answer. However, complete freedom of choice on all levels is not possible either. High-rises located in black areas, for example, can be operated successfully providing that the type and size of tenancy and the degree of high-rise is controlled. Similarly, large families can be accommodated, as well as 'broken' families, but there must also be a programme of controlled tenancy. With this type of tenancy the project should be in low-rise buildings, not too large, preferably located in outlying areas. Low-income families and socially unbalanced families can be housed together effectively, but there is a 'tipping point' and it is a fairly low one. If such families are admitted, the number must be controlled and unreasonable disruption must be cause for eviction. No community, in either public or private housing, can exist, irrespective of the amount of services provided, if serious anti-social behaviour is allowed to flourish on any significant scale.

There must be a controlled mix of conditions in order for public housing to survive and progress. Finally, in order to serve the many poor families who need housing, sufficient housing must be built so that 'socially unbalanced' families may be adequately served without too many being in any one project.

One of the unanswered questions raised by all social workers is where are you going to put the 'poor families' if you want to re-locate them out of an existing project. The experience of Patrick Feeney, Director of the Housing Authority of Columbus, Ohio, is instructive. Sawyer Homes contained two high-rise buildings with three, four and five bedroom units, each building housing about 150 families. Ninety-eight per cent of the families were black, many of them receiving public assistance to support large numbers of children. This repeated the pattern of many public housing projects in the USA. The problem, according to the Columbus Authority, was not enough play space for the children and not enough housing for the elderly. Actually the problems were far deeper than this but the Columbus Authority was able to persuade the community, black and white, of the necessity for dispersal of the project population into many areas of the city.

Columbus was not building much new family housing but they utilised their leasing programme which had 1,500 units available to relocate these project families.[5] So far, there have been no serious problems of community opposition which would overwhelm the Authority. Sawyer Homes was renovated into small units and was turned over to the elderly, changing the racial composition to about fifty-fifty black and white. At the same time, of course, the family composition changed from large families with many small children to elderly couples or single persons with no children. What the Columbus picture indicates is that families can be relocated and the existing projects re-used.

Another self-imposed stratification of tenants and tenant selection is found in the erection of special units for some married and single elderly. England, as well as Denmark, has for years recognised that older people have special needs. Years ago, flats or specially designed estates were built for the aged. After a while, however, it was recognised that older people are not satisfactorily housed in separate conglomerate dwellings. Large apartment buildings, tenanted exclusively by the aged, were often seen merely as stopping-off places before the cemetery. Separate projects for the elderly do, however, exist in the other countries. One such example is in Pepys's Estate of the Greater London Council, where there is a separate block of sixty flats for elderly tenants within a total project of 1,300 units. What is more typical, however, in Denmark, Holland, England and Israel, is a group of about ten flats set aside for older people, frequently on the ground floor of a larger apartment house. While there are administrative advantages in keeping larger groupings of older people together, they are not sufficiently important when other attendant problems are considered. The exception, of course, is invalids who require institutionalisation of a different type. In the United States there is a tendency to build exclusively for the elderly, as a substitute for building for low-income families.

A significant aspect of public housing in Europe is the architecture which is often indistinguishable from private housing. The structural similarity of private and public housing is explained by the fact that European countries, almost without exception, do not build a poverty appearance into their projects. Consequently, a broad spectrum of the population is attracted to public housing and waiting lists are usually long.

In New York City, with a long history of private high-rise buildings, public housing has been characterised by buildings somewhat similar in appearance to private housing. Although planners express concern over what such buildings do to the psyche of families, high-rise buildings have generally been well accepted by tenants and applicants. In England, too, planners inveigh against high-rise buildings and in the New Towns a concerted effort is made not to use these; although many New Towns like Thamesmead outside London, have moderate high-rises. In France, although high rises are built in considerable numbers, a frequent type is the four-storey two- and three-bedroom unit; but France, too, practises wide diversification in its housing. On the whole, where there are not other complicating factors—monotony, poverty-type architecture or socially unbalanced tenancy—the high-rise or middle-rise buildings seem to meet the needs adequately and continue to be built in considerable numbers as a necessary compromise to time, cost and location. Nevertheless, diversification of architecture, both in height and tenancy, is the desired goal.

Amenities in public housing are limited, since such projects operate on limited funds. However, limitation of funds in most European countries does not carry over an ideology that is reflected in building appearance. In many areas, public housing is built at considerably less expenditure per unit than private housing can build a similar type unit (and this is more true in Europe than in the United States). Projects are large, many including a thousand units and more, providing the advantages of large-scale buying. European and Israeli governments ask for, and receive, cheaper rates from building contractors. Land costs are driven down as the government uses the right of eminent domain. Better interest rates are made available, too. To some extent, cheaper materials are used where functional differences are minimal without labour or code considerations interfering.

Most projects suffer from serious apartment dimension limitations, but they have steadily increased in size. In Copenhagen, apartment sizes averaged 100 square metres. In 1948 in Israel, apartment sizes were an average of 48 square metres, while today they are upwards of 75 square metres per apartment. In the USSR, while average square metres per apartment are low, there have been marked increases since the beginning of the programme, averaging about 10 per cent more in the 1971 designs than pre-1960. In quite a few countries, while refrigerators, cooking and laundry facilities and central heating were not originally provided in public housing, the tendency today is to include many of these facilities. Where it is the custom of the country to omit such facilities, it does not seem to create the type of difference that distinguishes public housing from other types of housing or subjects tenants to invidious distinctions.

An important aspect of public housing in many countries is differing standards, not only from country to country but from period to period. In Israel, Puerto Rico and in the Soviet Union, significant changes took place from originally inadequate standards. One of the problems in the USA, where business interests are anxious not to have public housing built at all, is that their opposition is couched in terms of 'standards'. For example, unsympathetic interests contend on the one hand that public housing should not be built unless the technical 'standards' are satisfactory, then manage to have the government establish unreasonably high and rigid definitions of what is satisfactory, thus raising the necessary costs considerably above the prescribed maximums. On the other hand, the same group insists that no 'luxury' items or extras be included in poor people's housing. Again, this further retards the building of public housing.

To some extent standards are limiting in France where they are prescribed nationally, although they vary between types of housing. Nevertheless, most have modern amenities and none are poverty oriented. On the other hand, Israel and Puerto Rico (the latter being an exception to the American pattern) build housing they can afford and, as standards rise, build additional housing and attempt to replace older housing where it is inadequate. In Israel, immediately after the 1948 immigration, large amounts of *maabara* (temporary housing) were built, to accommodate the influx, but within twenty years these units have all been replaced. This type of adaptation of course occurs in the United States. In early public housing projects no closet doors, no toilet seat covers, stall showers as substitute for bath tubs and tiny bedrooms were all features of the programme. As the programme developed, many of these features were changed and while more recent projects do not have these limitations the poverty orientation still remains.

Project densities are high in public housing in Europe but, as in Holland with 970 people to the square mile, this is not considered a serious drawback. As much open space as possible is provided. In London, Copenhagen and Tel Aviv project densities are high and the amounts of recreational or open areas are admittedly not adequate, though in London and Copenhagen there are large amounts of open park space. High-rise buildings are common, but some control on tenancy types is maintained. It is recognised that high-rise buildings are not an answer for low-income, immigrant, large, or socially maladjusted families, but that some such buildings must be built if urban families are to be housed. While small family housing units with gardens are desirable, the amount of total space per unit, particularly public space, is of lesser importance. Therefore, many of the new housing projects have a higher land coverage than has traditionally been desirable, but it is considered a reasonable compromise between building in outlying areas or building high-rise buildings. Another important element is the number of smaller units provided— one and two bedroom units—what the British call 'bed-sitters', which reduces density in terms of people though not units.

Generally speaking, many of the projects in Europe are 300 to 500 units in size, but in England, France and Germany, for example, many estates of 1,000 to 1,500 units exist, with more being built.

Attempts are made to diversify the type of building and tenancy, with two-storey, four-storey and eight- to twelve-storey buildings being included. When middle-rise buildings are constructed, as in the high density Westminster housing estate, Lillington, 750 units are built but they are planned to accommodate 1,700 people, within a ten-acre area, or seventy-five families (170 persons) to the acre.

An important element of European housing is the emphasis on planning and the frequency with which plans are translated into action. Decisions as to height, type, location of buildings and number of rooms per unit, are generally made in European countries with some regard to community needs. Accommodation is considered in terms of economic realities but without the premise that public housing is an evil, and that the least amount built, in the most un-desirable location constitutes the greatest public good.

Edward Logue, of the New York State Urban Development Cor-poration, compared the powers of the USA and foreign planners. Logue says, 'Planners in the USA are relatively powerless in relation to the myriad of agencies responsible for carrying out or thwarting their recommendations. Elsewhere than the USA planners are seen as experts who make the consensus happen. In the USA they are irrelevant to the actual workings of the political processes.' In sum-ming up his remarks about planning of new communities he says that the 'great obstacles are fear, scepticism, fragmentation and a lack of commitment'. As an antidote, he recommends that local VIPs visit Stevenage (outside London), Vallingby (outside Stock-holm) and Tapiola (outside Helsinki).[6]

In the USA a cornerstone of its democracy is that such decisions be passed through legislative and administrative processes and the council of local businessmen exercise great influence over such decisions.* Occasionally, after a long period of gestation, this process may produce a token amount of public housing or generate a new panacea, such as turnkey housing, co-operative housing, union-sponsored housing, rent certifications or leasing of old housing—but all in driblets. Eternal vigilance on the part of the business com-munity and the necessary steps towards each accomplishment, ostensibly to insure democracy but in reality to insure inaction, is

* As recently as April 1971 the US Supreme Court validated a number of State laws enabling referenda in local communities that were designed to keep out public housing by local public demand.

enough to throttle any real housing programme. Should a programme, by some quirk, get going, it is crushed quickly.*

Moreover, public housing planning in Europe dovetails with
transportation, education and employment planning. In Israel it is
a national policy that the planning of housing is second only to
defence needs. And, equally important, housing is considered in
terms of dispersion, integration, provision for employment opportunity, factory development and all other aspects of community life.

In Britain, planning is oriented towards the welfare of the population rather than the individual needs of any one group. In its relocation of families the British government, nevertheless, takes the
position of urging, rather than the authoritative decision practised in
some Eastern European countries, or the somewhat insistent urging
in Israel of recent immigrants. Relatively few new towns developed
in the United States are planned in the sense that planners devised
Greenbelt, Maryland; Reston, Virginia; Columbia, Maryland,
as models to be emulated. Park Forest, Illinois and Levittown,
Pennsylvania are two examples of successful new towns. A large
number of suburbs have burgeoned since 1945, with almost no planning other than business considerations. New towns, in the European
sense of being specifically planned and governmentally organised,
have not materialised significantly. In the United States, new settlements are created out of the entrepreneurial tenacity and willing-
ness to gamble on the part of a contractor or promoter. But, as too
often has been the case, when the gamble fails, while the private
investors lose money, the residents lose far more.

Terence Bendixson, the author of the British chapter, contends that
the New Town programme is the finest accomplishment of the British
housing system of recent years. Israel believes that its dispersion
programme of immigrants is its greatest success. Yet both countries
recognise short-comings in their programmes. In Britain, middle
and upper classes have moved to the new towns, such as Stevenage,
whereas the lower-middle class and poorer families have tended to

---

* A good example of this occurred in 1965 in Chicago when a new programme
of buying up deteriorating housing in old neighbourhoods was put into effect by
a municipal agency with a vigorous executive. The programme proceeded for a
year and it seemed as if something might be accomplished, in a small way, to put
a large number of renovated houses at the disposal of the low-income community.
But the programme was discouraged and the executive released. A much more
significant cutback was the programme of moderate-income subsidies which
brought forth more than half a million new units under the Federal government
programme from 1969 to 1972. In 1973, this programme was cut off completely.

remain in the cities. Israel, on the other hand, has the problem of persuading doctors, lawyers, teachers, engineers, architects and musicians to move into outlying settlements. The settlements, of course, are different from the New Town suburbs of Britain. They are also more primitive than the New Towns established in Norway, Sweden, West Germany and Finland. The latter more closely resemble American suburbs, without 'planned exclusivity', and are organised by the government, which owns the land and plans for employment, schools, shopping centres, health centres and recreational activity.

As Johann Wolfgang Werner points out in the article on union housing in West Germany, numerous new towns or suburbs have come into being in West Germany, such as Munich-Perlach and Hohnercamp. These also resemble American suburbs such as Park Forest and Levittown, though they may also possess some of the best characteristics of Vallingsby and Skarholmen. They are completely planned by the local and provincial government in conjunction with the Urban Renewal and Planning section (NHS) of Neue Heimat.

The greatest number of New Towns has been built in the USSR where from 1921 to 1969 it is reported that 934 new cities and towns came into being. In the post-war period as many as 100 to 125 new cities sprang up every five years. These are new towns with full public sponsorship and backing, attempting to serve in an embryo way the industrial, educational, housing, health and cultural needs. Here, indeed, the force of the government is felt. Many industrial towns, resort towns and towns of every description have been developed with government planning, placing emphasis on developing unsettled areas of the country. This has required an authoritarianism and disregard of personal and individual preference and involved considerable personal dislocations. In Sweden and Israel, too, complaints of authoritarianism and disregard of individual needs are frequently made; but the question becomes one of degree and priority.

In all these countries, planning considerations are not the sole province of the central government. In Britain, borough planning is of enormous importance. In Israel, at least in recent years, local governments are given more importance and central government plans now have to be submitted to local administrations in Tel Aviv, Haifa and Jerusalem for approval. While plans are not submitted to the citizenry in these locations, the individual interests of localities are considered. As discussed in the Swedish and Israeli chapters, this is one of the more knotty problems that planners have to face; the problem of balance, not only between what the locality as a government authority wishes, but what individual citizen groups desire and what seems best in terms of allocation of limited community resources.

The question of citizen participation is a particularly sensitive one in public housing development and placement. In Puerto Rico, for example, former Director of the Housing Authority, Carlos Alvarado, points out that tenants and prospective neighbourhoods are a significant factor in the making of housing decisions. In New York City, citizens' groups are encouraged and utilised, according to the administrator, in making administrative decisions. On the other hand, occasionally such groups become dominated by organisations and individuals with disruptive aims whose interests do not coincide with their own community, the larger community, or even the tenancy. In any such case, whether in Israel, New York City, Puerto Rico or England, it becomes difficult, if not dangerous, to allow such groups to dominate.* As Israel Shaham explains, 'Sometimes in new settlements, local citizenry have to be permitted to make their own decisions and their own mistakes; at least as to certain facets of the programme'. As planners in England and Israel indicate, it may be important psychologically to listen to the views of such groups but the final consideration upon which decisions are made about which plans are drawn up and carried out should be made by administrative heads taking into consideration the needs of the tenants, that of the surrounding neighbourhood, and that of the underlying community.

Inextricably bound up with a planning and housing programme is the land policy. In the United States, the land policy has been

---

* A prime example of the irresponsibility of some citizen groups was reported in the Pittsburgh newspapers in September 1969, which unanimously condemned the actions. The Housing Authority had been asked to transfer a tenant from a leased unit to a project apartment and was unable to do it for administrative reasons. The citizen group, led by the local director of VISTA, Richard Ridenour, stormed into the commissioner's meeting and demanded to be heard. The Executive Director Alfred J. Tronso patiently listened to the complaint and then asked them to leave while the matter as well as others were to be discussed. Ridenour managed to get close to the Executive Director and handcuffed him to the tenant saying that 'unless the Housing Authority agreed to give the family a unit they would have to stay manacled together'. While the action was outrageous and universally berated, especially so in view of the enlightened position of this administration, what it says about the behaviour of 'irresponsible' citizen groups is more unsettling. How far can well-meaning administrators go with such groups!

governed by the enormous amount of land available and the seeming lack of need to control the use of such land. The European and Israel experience make it clear that social land control, as contrasted with the practice of zoning and its exceptions, is the only answer to the urban housing problems. The extent to which land control, in the hands of real estate interests, operating through municipal government, can stymy public housing is apparent in almost any metropolis which has tried to establish a genuine public housing programme.

In the United States most public housing has been placed in slums and by and large rejected for outlying areas. In Europe much housing is built in outlying areas, so that it can be built without waiting for the slum areas to be acquired and razed, although development plans are also made for central urban areas, particularly to clear up war-damaged areas and to revive old areas. In Hungary, for example, the renewal of town centre areas is a much more expensive programme; hence, the concentration is on vacant sites.

In France, through a series of regulations, the government controls any mass building in outlying areas by private developers. All building must be cleared with the municipality and the regional representatives of the government; and approval follows only if the development plan is in accord with the governmental plan for the area. Likewise in Germany, Neue Heimat as well as local government generally takes the position that housing must be built on outlying land, where it is relatively inexpensive and available.

Britain, which has built on outlying vacant land for years, however, recognises that a considerable amount of building must go on in the inner city, together with slum clearance and urban renewal. The local boroughs in London, which build almost 50 per cent more housing annually than the Greater London Council, build a substantial amount of their housing on cleared land. Both an inner-city building programme and a vacant land programme are necessary.

In Israel the government owns 97 per cent of the land and leases some of it to private organisations and individuals that wish to develop it for industrial, residential or commercial purposes. In Scandinavian countries the government is empowered to buy land, on the basis that ultimately the government will use it or lease it out. This solution keeps speculation under control. A similar programme was adopted by Puerto Rico under Governor Munoz Marin; and a programme of land control and land purchase is also operative in France.

The attitude towards land control is also reflected in the policy towards properties in private hands. In Scandinavia, West Germany and England, if properties are not maintained they are often taken over by the government, at land or site value.

In Denmark, when land comes onto the market that the city would like for its own plans, the government bids for it and does not concern itself with temporary losses in taxes nor the alternative possible use for such land by private businesses.

In several countries, Denmark, Sweden and West Germany, co-operative housing is the type of non-profit housing utilised rather than publicly operated units. In some of these countries, notably France and Israel, public housing shares the stage with co-operative housing. The proportion of housing built or sponsored by co-operative tenant associations or housing corporations of a non-profit nature has increased enormously in the last twenty-five years. In Sweden it currently accounts for just over half of the housing units built. In Denmark approximately 30 per cent of the units are co-operatively operated and in Israel there is an equally substantial proportion. In West Germany co-operative and non-profit housing amount to about one-quarter of the housing stock and two-fifths of the current production.

There is considerable overlap between 'co-operative housing' and housing built by unions. In Denmark trade unions and trade union members are very active in workers' co-operative movements. The difference between co-operative housing and union-sponsored housing, in both the type of housing and the families to whom the housing is directed, is not great and depends in part on historical accidents and the extent and nature of union development. It appears obvious that in countries without a well-developed consumer co-operative movement, a logical focal point for such development would be the union, since co-operative efforts often lack the expertise or motivation to carry through an extensive housing programme.

Successful housing co-operative associations are usually worker-oriented organisations that owe their success to governmental subsidies including long-term amortisation of capital investment and the economies of large-scale purchasing power, as well as the non-profit nature of the organisations.

In Hungary and the USSR building by co-operatives is growing at a great pace and is being encouraged by the state. In these countries it becomes a way in which the professional and industrial classes can obtain better housing and have a greater stake in it. For the country, it provides a method of saving important amounts of down payments which are made by the individual out of personal savings rather than by the government.

The two countries in which labour union federations are most effective in building for low- and moderate-income families are Israel and West Germany.

The United States, in contrast, with some 18 million members active in labour unions, builds very little housing through such organisations. From 1945 to the beginning of 1971, 100,000 units of housing were built through labour unions, and most of these were in New York City, sponsored by social welfare-minded labour unions. Several attempts have been made in Chicago but only one has recently come to fruition, that of the Amalgamated Clothing Workers Union.

In Israel, one of the biggest builders and developers is Histradrut, the workers' federation. Projects built and frequently operated by the Histradrut can be seen throughout Israel. In West Germany, Neue Heimat is the organisation in which German labour unions vested the power for building and planning of housing. In all, Neue Heimat has built over 400,000 units in West Germany, mostly since 1945. These unions operate in much the same way as co-operatives as far as building arrangements are concerned. They use financial aids, planning considerations and management inducements. Their rentals are low and they are designed to serve low- and moderate-income families. The fundamental principle in both union and co-operative housing movements is that the housing must be produced efficiently, at low cost, with no profit, and that they must supply low-rent housing for workers.

Industrialised housing has its greatest use in the Soviet Union. It is the prime means through which most of the housing is being built and it is being built in huge quantities. Russians will admit, and critics are quick to notice, that as the result of the very rapid building in the Soviet Union, with low but continuously increasing standards, a number of individual benefits are lost and that much of the housing has a somewhat shoddy quality shortly after it is built. In the Soviet Union prefabrication has taken hold because of the savings in economic cost, labour cost and time. It is no longer a question of programming or whether to invest in prefabricated housing but rather 'what kind'. For example, in the Russian cities, 70 per cent of

7

the building is in pre-cast concrete. The question today is: should such prefabrication be of pre-cast concrete wall panels or should the apartment house be built in a series of finished 'boxes' put in place by huge cranes? The answer lies in production and transport. The box method is much more difficult to transport and must be manufactured relatively close to site. Another difficulty in this type of building is relative uniformity and lack of diversity of architecture. This is reported to be gradually improving. The biggest single deficiency in the Russian building seems to be the lack of quality control. In some other countries, such as Sweden and Israel, there is also a good deal of dissatisfaction with prefabricated housing as it is currently being produced. This does not mean that unhappiness with their current mode of housing production is particularly prevalent, although it undoubtedly exists in considerable measure. What it does mean in Sweden, USSR and Israel, is that although housing has a high priority, it does not displace industry, health or education and in most countries it is very secondary to defence. Competition from other national priorities frequently forces housing standards to a considerably less than ideal level.

Perhaps the most important indication for the future is the way in which industrialised building has been accepted, both in Israel and in the USSR, and in Sweden, West Germany and France as well. In the five countries where planning had a solid voice and where building housing seems to be all-important, such industrialisation exists to a high degree. In the United States, the federal government has conducted a pilot programme known as 'Operation Break Through' as an experiment in system-built housing. Different methods are used in each city and although the programme is not calculated to upset any existing apple carts, some progress seems to be in the making.

One of the important alternatives to public housing building even more frequently mentioned in the USA is that of direct subsidies. Housing subsidies have been used for many years in France, West Germany, Denmark and Britain, but they are used with public or non-profit housing, not instead of it. In Britain, for example, 'fair' rents are set by the GLC at what might be termed a net cost basis. However, since using a net cost places rents too high for many, tenant subsidies are then given, depending on size of family and the type of unit, to reduce the rent to manageable proportions. Essentially the same principle is used in West Germany for the rental housing which constitutes the bulk of Neue Heimat production. Subsidies are given to building promoters to reduce cost and also to tenants depending on income and apartment size. The same policy is followed with variations in France and in Denmark. Consequently, there is nothing in the history of public housing that contradicts the use of subsidies and, in some circumstances, they are advisable along with the use of public or non-profit housing.

In the USA subsidies have been utilised in the last few years to build moderate-income housing. The subsidies have the purpose of bringing down the interest cost from market interest to 1 per cent per year and are available in houses or flats for families with incomes around $6,000 and somewhat higher. Families with lower incomes cannot afford the housing because the rent-income ratio is too high although in a few instances the programme is combined with rent supplements.

The great problem in the USA is that even with subsidies, private enterprise has found out how to milk the government by using the buildings as tax shelters, building inferior apartments in the poorest areas and, when the buildings fail, leaving the government to pick up the pieces.

In instances where local housing authorities in the USA have got into economic difficulties, although subsidies have never been used in this way in the USA, it would certainly seem preferable to fill vacancies with slightly higher income tenants, raise the rents and give subsidies to those who cannot afford increases, rather than tear the projects down.

The need for subsidies is in part dependent upon the desired rent-income ratios, or the proportion of income that should be paid as rent. In USSR, 5 to 6 per cent of income is paid as rent; in Denmark it is just under 20 per cent; it is 15 to 18 per cent in West Germany; the figures vary considerably by country and by time, depending on what is included in rent. Altogether the proportion paid by European countries is less than in the USA despite the fact that many real estate specialists urge that the United States population would get better housing if only they paid a still larger proportion of their income for housing.

Many questions are raised about ownership versus rental of housing. In Britain there has been an increase in the number of dwellings that can be sold to the tenants since the Conservative government came into office. Nonetheless, the Greater London

Council continued to limit the number of dwellings that may be sold in any one project to 12 per cent. The trend away from rentals in Britain is not marked and it appears that rental housing will continue strongly for a considerable period of time, particularly since in the last two years the rental supply market for private dwellings has been sharply reduced and the prices of private rental housing have rocketed.

In France the bulk of housing is rental housing, as is true in Neue Heimat programmes in West Germany, but there is a trend in the direction of more owned flats. In Sweden and Denmark the same trends are apparent. All in all, while there is a considerable amount of housing being constructed for owner-occupiers (for example, 20 per cent and more in West Germany and France) European planners recognise that national economic questions plus the desire of people to concentrate in bigger cities require the bulk of housing to be rental housing at moderate and low-rent levels.

In Israel much of the earlier public housing had been operated on a rental basis. In recent years a marked trend towards ownership of housing has occurred. It was believed important to have people save and contribute to the upkeep of their flats. Most of Israel's building is in multi-family units and is in the ownership category. Nevertheless, everything is done by the government to insure that anyone in need can obtain a flat if they cannot raise a sufficient down payment. In the newer housing the emphasis has been on ownership with long-term mortgages, low interest and down payments. However, as pointed out in the Israel chapter, when down payments are reduced further and terms liberalised, the difference between rental and ownership becomes minimal as far as upkeep attitudes are concerned. While the system of tenant ownership of flats is widespread in Israel, many more doubts are now being raised against the principle.

To own means to invest materially. If the investment is too large, poorer tenants cannot buy in or believe that the government is taking advantage of them. If it is too low and monthly payments are high with growth of equity low, tenants feel put upon and resent the government. Ownership can become a fiction. Again ownership can inhibit employment mobility and in a country such as Israel, employment and mobility has a meaning of its own. If as in the past there is no fixed amortisation rate and the rate fluctuates with cost of living, the owner builds up even less equity with increasing monthly payments. This has created huge dissatisfactions and a feeling that the occupant has been defrauded.

A recent discussion regarding public housing with a Spanish expert indicated that Spain had had the same experience as Israel with its home ownership programme. The flats were sold to the residents because this seemed a better alternative, but because of the small rent and small down payment and long amortisation period little equity was built up after ten years and owners were dissatisfied. Moreover, the mass housing of an earlier period, of a low standard, was no longer adequate for the residents whose families had grown, and whose standards had risen. When these owners found it difficult to sell the flats, and received no equity, they were bitter in their denunciation of the government. Thus, although the programme of ownership is still sizeable and is growing in some quarters, such as Great Britain, there is also a noticeable slowing down of the process in other countries and a recognition of the great need for rental housing for the moderate- and low-income sectors.

In summary, whether ownership or rental housing is preferable for the large masses of middle- and low-income families who require housing is by no means a settled question, and there are trends and counter-trends. Whether such housing is best provided by direct government involvement, by co-operative sponsorship, or by unions, is likewise not clear. Whether the means through which money should be channelled is by tax reductions, by producer or consumer subsidies, or by direct government grants has not been crystallised. All have been used at different places and times with moderately good effect. What does seem clear is that the free swinging private business activities which characterised the nineteenth and much of the twentieth centuries in the area of home building are no longer possible if our cities are to continue to be places of continued vitality. Cities and national governments must make meaningful plans for building for the whole population even where such plans are to be carried through by the private sector. Further, it is recognised in virtually all advanced countries, socialist or not, that there must be large-scale governmental involvement in the planning, promoting and financing of housing for a large segment of the population.

NOTES

1. Ministry of Housing in Denmark, *Housing in Nordic Countries*, p. 40 ff.
2. Ascher, Charles, *The Administration of Publicly Aided Housing*, 1971, p. 28.
3. Newman, M. W., *Chicago Daily News*, 24 June 1971, Interview with New York City Housing Authority.
4. Urban Renewal and Housing Corporation, *A Plan and Recommended Program for the Transformation of Nemesio Canales*, San Juan, 1967.
5. An interview with Patrick Feeney in May, 1971.
6. Logue, Edward, 'Piecing the Political Pie', *Saturday Review*, (15 May 1971).

Selected Bibliography

GENERAL WORKS: USA

Burns, Leland S. et al. *Housing: Symbol and Shelter.* A report prepared for and submitted to the Agency for International Development. Los Angeles: University of California, 1970.

Business Week. 'The Bankruptcy of Subsidized Housing.' 27 May 1972.

Canty, Donald (ed.) *Urban America: The Ill Housed.* A compendium of recent writings and reports on national housing policy. Prepared for the League of Women Voters. Washington, DC, 1969.

Congressional Quarterly. 'Growing Issue: Communities *vs.* Low Income Housing.' 8 January 1972, pp. 51–5.

Fried, Joseph. 'Any Hope for Housing?' *Saturday Review,* 12 February 1972.

Fried, Joseph. 'Simeon Golar's City-Within-a-City.' *New York Times Magazine,* 30 April 1972.

Frieden, Bernard and Joann Newman. 'Home Ownership for the Poor.' *Transaction,* October 1970, pp. 47–53.

Goodwin, Richard. 'Now There's a New Way to Kill Housing with the Sacred Cry of Pollution.' *Professional Builder,* December 1969.

Goldberg, Abba Arthur. 'State Agencies: Housing Assistance at the Grass Roots.' *Real Estate Review,* Winter 1972.

Gruen, Niva Joffe. *Low and Moderate Income Housing in the Suburbs.* New York: Praeger, 1972.

House and Home. 'Five Projects Show That the Best of Today's Subsidized Housing is Very Good Indeed.' February 1972.

Jacobs, Jane. *Death and Life of Great American Cities.* New York: Vintage Books, 1961.

Journal of Home Building. 'Low Income Housing: Total Involvement Is Key to Success'. May 1971, pp. 40–42.

Lalli, Frank. 'Scandal in Chicago—State Probes Fiasco in Housing the Poor.' *House and Home,* August 1969.

Lansing, Jack, Charles Clifton and James N. Morgan. *New Homes and Poor People: A Study of Chains.* Institute for Social Research. Ann Arbor: University of Michigan Press, 1969.

Ledbetter, William H. *Public Housing: A Social Experiment Seeks Acceptance*. Seminar on Law and Contemporary Problems. Durham: Duke University, 1967.

Lindsay, John V. 'Housing and the Federal Government.' *Mortgage Banker*, May 1970, pp. 28–9.

Meyerson, Martin and Ed Banfield. *Politics, Planning and the Public Interest*. Free Press, 1955.

Mitchell, Robert Edward. 'Some Social Implications of High Density Housing.' *American Sociological Review*, February 1971.

Morton, Jane. 'Paying for Housing.' *RIBA Journal*, September 1971, pp. 401–2.

Nenno, Mary K. 'A Year of Truth for the Future Course of Urban Affairs.' *Journal of Housing*, February–March 1972, pp. 61–8.

Newman, Oscar. *Defensible Space*. New York: Macmillan, 1972.

Ontario Housing. 'Public Housing Tenants Are Part of Community.' Ontario: December 1971.

Peel, N., G. E. Pickett and S. T. Buehl. 'Racial Discrimination in Public Housing Site Selection.' *Stanford Law Review*, Vol. 23. November 1970.

Piven, Frances Fox and Richard Cloward. 'Desegregating Housing.' *New Republic*, 17 December 1966.

Professional Builder. 'Inner City Apartments Overcome Ghetto Label, Revive Old Neighborhood.' June 1971, p. 147.

Racster, R., H. C. Smith and W. B. Brueggeman. 'Federal Housing Programs in the Local Housing Market.' *The Appraisal Journal*, Vol. XXXIX. July 1971, pp. 396–414.

Rainwater, Lee. *Behind Ghetto Walls: Black Families in a Federal Slum*. Chicago: Aldine Press, 1970.

Rose, Albert. 'Canadians Are Among the Best Housed People in the World.' *Ontario Housing*, June 1970.

Schorr, Alvin. *Slums and Social Insecurity*. US Dept. of Health and Welfare, Research Report No. 1. Washington: US Government Printing Office, 1963.

Spolan, Herman S. 'The Case for Variable Rate Review.' *Real Estate Review*, Vol. I. Summer 1971, pp. 15–18.

Starr, Roger. 'The Lesson of Forest Hills.' *Commentary*. June 1972.

Starr, Roger. 'Which of the Poor Shall Live in Public Housing?' *Public Interest*, Spring 1971.

Strauss, Nathan. *Two Thirds of a Nation: A Housing Program.* New York: Alfred A. Knopf, 1952.

Taggart, Robert, III. *Low Income Housing: A Critique of Federal Aid.* Baltimore: Johns Hopkins Press, 1970.

Thaler, David G. 'Government Subsidized Housing: Sleeper Market of the 70s.' *House and Home.* December 1970, pp. 53–61.

Wenzlick, Ray. 'As I See It the HUD Subsidy Program Is an Expensive Failure.' *Real Estate Analyst,* April 1972.

Wilfield, Thad. 'Housing Problem: American *vs.* the European Experience.' *Public Interest,* Spring 1972, pp. 78–95.

SPECIAL WORKS

Co-operatives

Architectural Forum. 'Design for 1600 East Harlem Cooperative Project Has Emerged from Administrative Limbo in Completely Revised Form.' May 1971.

Chapman, Stanley. *The History of Working-class Housing: A Symposium.* Rossman & Littlefield, 1971.

Heinen, B. *Contribution of Cooperative Housing Societies to the Solution of Technical and Social Problems of Urbanization.* New York: United Nations Document, 1969.

House and Home. 'Condominiums Go Sour Without Professional Management.' June 1972.

Kleinman, Rose. 'Labor Co-ops Join in Programs for Making Jobs, Homes.' *Cooperative Housing,* Fall 1964.

Liblit, Jerome. *Housing the Cooperative Way* (selected readings), New York: Twayne, 1964.

Perring, Michael. 'An Appraisal of Some New Co-ownership Schemes.' *Housing Review,* July–August 1969.

Repps, Saul M. 'Low Income Co-ops Need Professional Management.' *Journal of Property Management.* May–June 1972.

Teaford, Stephen D. 'Home Ownership for Low Income Families: The Condominium.' *Hastings Law Journal,* Vol. 21. 1970, pp. 243–286.

US Dept. of Housing & Urban Development: Office of International Affairs. *Cooperative Housing.* Prepared for Agency for International Development. Washington, DC, 1971.

Voorhis, Jerry. 'The Hope of Housing.' *The Progressive.* October 1971.

New Towns

Alonzo, William. 'The Mirage of New Towns.' *The Public Interest*, Spring 1970, pp. 3–17.

Building Research. 'New Towns: Frontiers or Failures.' October–December 1970 (entire issue).

Davie, Leonard. 'Vision or Hoax: The New Town Mirage.' *Nation*, 15 May 1972.

Dertbick, Martha. *New Towns in Town. Why a Federal Program Failed*. Washington: Urban Institute, 1970.

Frederick, Brian. 'The Legality of Affirmative Measures to Achieve and Maintain Integration in a New Town.' *Georgetown Law Journal*, 1970–71, pp. 335–63.

House and Home. 'Nuns Island—A New Standard for High Density Communities.' December 1969, pp. 56–63.

Lambeth, Edmund. 'New Towns, Can They Work?' *Washington Monthly*, October 1969.

Lichfield, Nathaniel and Paul F. Wendt. 'Six English New Towns, A Financial Analysis.' *Town Planning Review*, October 1969, pp. 283–314.

Logue, Edward J. 'Piecing the Political Pie.' *Saturday Review*. 15 May 1971.

Luden, Gwen. 'Conserve and Rehabilitate.' *Building*, 2 January 1970, pp. 29–30.

Naftalin, Arthur. 'Minneapolis: A Case Study in a Unified Attack on Urban Problems.' *Journal of Housing*, December 1969.

Powledge, Frank. 'New Haven: Triumph and Trouble in Model City.' *Washington Monthly*, February 1970.

Town and Country Planning. New Towns Issue. January 1972.

Saturday Review, 'New Communities, A Symposium,' 15 May 1971.

EUROPEAN WORKS

Denmark

Borsing, Vaj. *Danish Town Planning*. Copenhagen: Ministry of Housing, 1966.

Christiansen, Kai. 'Ideas About Houses of the Future.' *Build International*, October 1969, pp. 23–5.

Denmark: Bolig Ministeriet. *The Proposed Reform of the Danish Land Use Legislation*. Copenhagen: 1969.

Denmark: Ministry of Housing. *Current Trends and Policies in the Field of Housing, Building and Planning in Denmark.* Copenhagen: 1969.

Denmark: Ministry of Housing. *Danish Housing Requirements, 1960–80.* Copenhagen: 1965.

Denmark: Ministry of Housing. *Danish Non-Profit Housing with Common Service Facilities.* Copenhagen: May 1968.

Denmark: Ministry of Housing. *Housing in the Nordic Countries by the Ministry of Housing and Others.* Copenhagen: 1968.

Denmark: Ministry of Housing. *Housing Problems of the Physically Handicapped.* Copenhagen: February 1966.

Denmark: Ministry of Housing. *One Family Housing in Denmark.* Copenhagen: November 1960.

Denmark: Ministry of Housing. *Role of Government and Service Organizations in the Field of Industrialized Housing.* Copenhagen: July 1968.

Engberg, Einar, Chief of Section, Denmark: Ministry of Housing. *Special Housing Requirements for the Elderly and the Handicapped.* World Health Organization, June 1961.

Grue. *Danish Mortgage System Housing Mortgage Funds of Denmark.* Ministry of Housing. Copenhagen: September 1965.

Kjeldsen, M. *Long Term Planning and Industrialization of Housebuilding in Denmark.* Ministry of Housing. Copenhagen: February 1965.

France

Cabane, Mirelle, *Le Financement du Logement en France.* Secrétariat Général du Gouvernement. Paris: July 1970.

Cahiers du Centre Scientifique et Technique du Botment. *Matériaux Varieux et Procèdes Non-traditionel de Construction.* No. 104. November 1969.

Claudins-Petit, M. Eugene. 'Loger la Famille dans la Ville.' *L'Habitat.* June 1969, pp. 53–6.

Fondation Nationale des Sciences Politiques. *L'Expérience Française de Villes Nouvelles.* Paris: 1970.

France: Bureau d'Etudes et Réalisations Urbaines. *Evolution et Transformation du Site Comme Facteurs dans le Phénomène d'Urbanisation.* Paris: 1969.

Holden, Constance. 'French Experiment in Urbanization without Tears.' *Science*, 1 October 1971, pp. 39–42.

Housing Review. 'The Hard Core of the Housing Problem.' Report of the Housing Centre Annual Conference. September–October 1971, pp. 119–38.

L'Habitation. 'La Participation du Public.' June 1969, pp. 38–42.

Ministère du Logement. Livre Blanc. Paris: September 1970.

Ministère de L'Equipment et du Logement. *Urbanisme*. Paris; June 1970.

Rapoport, Amos. 'Housing and Housing Densities in France.' *Town Planning Review*. January 1969, pp. 341–54.

Sheers, P. A. 'Planning City Regions in France and Great Britain.' *Town Planning Institute Journal*. November 1971.

Soolman, Howard. *Haussman: Paris Transformed*. New York: George Brazillier, 1971.

Villes Nouvelles. 'L'Architecture d'Aujourdhui.' October–November 1969, pp. 3–102. (English summaries.)

Germany

Dietrichs, H. E. *Non-Profit Housing Enterprises in the Federal Republic of Germany*. Hamburg: George August Walter's Druckerei, 1969.

Doring, Wolfgang. 'Raumstellen.' *Neue Heimat*, December 1969.

Dornhoff, George. 'Das Eindhoven Beispiel.' *Neue Heimat*, March 1970, pp. 1–8.

Feuerstein, Günther. *New Directions in German Architecture*. New York, George Brazillier, 1968.

Hamilton, Calvin. 'If the Germans Can Do It, Better City Planning, More Controls Offer Lessons for the U.S.' *Landscape Architecture*, April 1972.

Neue Heimat. 'Low Cost Housing and the Trade Unions.' Hamburg: 1963. (English summary.)

Neue Heimat. Report of General Development of the Housing and Construction Economy from Operating Report of 1965 of Neue Heimat. Hamburg: 1965.

Neue Heimat. 'Von Hannibal bis Asenwald: A Cooperative Housing Project 6 km. from Stuttgart.' Hamburg: November 1968.

Schneider, Gottfried. *Housing Cooperatives in the Federal Republic of Germany*. Gesamtverband Gemeinnutziger Wohnungs Unternehmen. Cologne: July 1969.

Great Britain

Broady, Maurice. *Planning for People. Essays on the Social Centre of Planning*. National Council of Social Service. London: Bedford Square Press, 1968.

Cocks, Freda. 'Housing Allowances for Private Tenants. Birmingham's Experiences.' *Housing Review*. January–February 1972.

Cook, Franklin H. 'Public Ownership: United Kingdom *vs*. U.S.' *Public Utilities Fortnightly*, 18 December 1969, pp. 26–34.

Crofton, B. A. 'Statistical Assessment of Housing Need.' *Housing*, January 1972, pp. 7–10.

Gilmour, Andrew. 'Council Housing and Cooperative Ownership.' *Housing Review*. May–June 1969, pp. 84–9.

Greater London Council. *Planning of a New Town*. Data and design based on a study for a New Town of 100,000 at Hook, Hampshire. London: 1965.

Housing. 'Housing Advice Centre, Lambeth.' July 1970.

Lever, W. F. 'Planning Standards and Residential Densities.' *Town Planning Institute Journal*, November 1971, pp. 400–403.

Municipal and Public Services Journal. 'Liverpool Tackles Its Big Slum Problem.' 15 August 1969, p. 2065 ff.

Naismith, R. J. 'Scotland's Towns are Centuries New'. *Architect*, August 1971, pp. 25–8.

Nevitt, Adela A. 'The New Housing Legislation.' *Housing Review*, March–April 1972, pp. 60–63.

Reubens, Edwin P. 'Our Urban Ghettos in British Perspectives.' *Urban Affairs Quarterly*, March 1971, pp. 319–40.

Richardson, Harry W. *Housing in the 70s: Projection and Policy*. Centre for Research in the Social Sciences. University of Kent: 1970.

Tarn, J. M. 'Housing in Liverpool and Glasgow.' *Town Planning Review*, January 1969, pp. 310–34.

Taylor, Alan. 'Local Authority Housing in Scotland.' *RIBA Journal*, February 1971, pp. 68–72.

US News and World Report. 'What America Can Learn from Britain's "New Towns."' 20 September 1971, pp. 61–3.

Hungary

Economist. 'All Eyes on Hungary's Houses.' 12 June 1971, p. 36 ff.

Hungary: University of Building & Urban Development. *Actual Trends and Policies in Housing, Building, Industry and Planning in the Hungarian People's Republic.* Document HOU/141. Budapest: 1969.

Israel

Baruch, Nissim. *Housing in Israel.* Ministry of Housing, June 1969.

Golani, Yehonathan. *Israel Builds: 1970.* Jerusalem: Ministry of Housing, 1970.

Israel: Ministry of Planning and Development. *A New Approach to Urban and Regional Planning.* Tel Aviv: 1968.

Israel: Ministry of Housing. *Housing in Relation to the National Level of Economic and Social Development in Israel.* Tel Aviv: May 1966.

Israel: Ministry of Housing. *Israel Builds: 1948–1968.* Tel Aviv: 1969.

Israel: Ministry of the Interior. *National Planning for the Redistribution of Population and the Establishment of New Towns in Israel.* Tel Aviv: 1964.

Marans, Robert W. 'Planning the Experimental Neighbourhood at Kiryat Gan.' *Ekistics,* 1969.

Morris, M. D. 'New Towns in the Desert.' *American City,* November 1970, pp. 94–6.

Netherlands

Decision Making and Functioning Principles of Housing. Rotterdam: Borecentrum, 1970.

Netherlands: Ministry of Housing. *Current Trends and Policies in the Field of Housing and Planning During the Year 1968.* The Hague: May 1969.

Netherlands: Ministry of Housing Information Service. *Housing of Elderly People of the Netherlands.* The Hague, 1969.

Netherlands: Ministry of Housing and Physical Planning. *Housing in the Netherlands.* The Hague: September 1966.

Netherlands: Ministry of Housing and Physical Planning. *The Picture of the Old Housing Stock for the Netherlands.* The Hague: 1970.

Puerto Rico

Reed, William V. and Frank Molther. 'New San Juan, An Unparalleled Opportunity.' *AIA Journal,* May 1970.

Rich (F. D.) Co. *Housing for 20,000 Individuals: A Proposal for Berwind, San Juan, Puerto Rico.* Designed by Victor Bisharat. San Juan.

Urban Renewal Administration. *Planning for Housing in Puerto Rico: A Social Approach.* San Juan: 1971.

USSR

Engineering News Record. 'Moscow's 30-Year Building Plan Puts Housing in the Lead Role.' 18 May 1972.

Herman, Leon M. 'Urbanization and New Construction in the Soviet Union.' *American Journal of Economics and Sociology.* April 1971, pp. 203–20.

H.U.D. Challenge. *Housing Construction in the U.S.S.R.* May 1971.

H.U.D. International Brief. *Housing Industry in the U.S.S.R.* March 1971.

Moskva Stroizdat. *Principles of Town Planning in the Soviet Union.* 1966, 1970. (Translated from Russian for the Department of H.U.D. and National Science Foundation by Indian National Scientific Documentation Centre.)

US News & World Report. 'Russia Takes a Census.' 18 May 1970, pp. 50–51.

Winkler, Jack. 'Russia Faces Up to the Realities of the Construction Industry in Reorganizing its Approach to Producing Housing.' *Architectural Record,* October 1969.

Wright, James R. *Industrialized Building in the Soviet Union.* U.S. Dept. of Commerce. Washington: U.S. Government Printing Office, 1971.

Spain

King, John C. 'Housing in Spain.' *Town Planning Review,* October 1971, pp. 381–402.

Spain: Ministerio de la Vivienda. *Evolution de la Vivienda en Espana en el Periodo 1953–1963.* Madrid, 1967.

Spain: Ministerio de la Vivienda. *Financiacion de la Construcion de Viviendas Sociales en Europe.* Madrid: 1969.

Spain: Ministerio de la Vivienda. *Informe a la Comision de Viviendas de las Cortes Antecedentes.* Madrid: 1971.

Sweden

Anton, Thomas J. 'Politics and Planning in a Swedish Suburb.' *American Institute of Planners Journal,* July 1969.

Engineering Construction World. 'New Stockholm Suburb to House 45,000.' February 1972, pp. 10–17.

Hutzen, Heikkia and Paul D. Spreirigen. *Building a New Town, Finland's New Garden City, Tapiola.* Cambridge, Mass.: Massachusetts Institute of Technology, 1971.

Lewis, Ralph. 'Something is Rotten in the State of Sweden.' *Architect,* May 1972.

Odivann, Ella. *Urbanization in Sweden.* News and Methods for Planning. Stockholm: 1970.

Sweden: National Housing Board. *Current Trends and Policies in the Field of Housing, Building and Planning.* Stockholm: 1970.

GENERAL: EUROPE

Abrams, Charles. *Man's Struggle for Shelter in an Urbanizing World.* Harper and Row, 1970.

Aronov, Edward. 'European Approach to Problem Families.' *Journal of Housing,* Vol. 14, No. 7, April 1957.

Ascher, Charles S. *The Administration of Publicly Aided Housing.* International Institute of Administrative Services, Martinus Nijhoff, The Hague, 1971.

Business Week. 'New Towns. The Lessons Europe is Teaching Us.' 22 November 1969.

Cibula, Evelyn. ' "Social" Housing in Europe.' *Building.* 21 April 1972, pp. 113–17.

Donnison, David V. *Government in Housing,* Penguin Books, 1967.

Falk, Karl L. *Housing Problems and Tax Policies, An International Comparison.* National Association of Housing and Redevelopment Officials, Washington, DC, December 1969.

Office of International Affairs, HUD. *Urban Growth Policies in Six European Countries.* A Report by the Urban Growth Policy Study Group, 23 August–10 September 1972.

Perkins, George. 'Low Rise Housing in Seven Countries,' *Housing Review,* March–April 1972.

Silverman, Abner, *Selected Aspects of Publicly Owned Housing: Great Britain, Netherlands and Sweden.* Housing and Home Finance Agency: January 1961.

Strong, Ann Louise. *Planned Urban Environments: Sweden, Finland, The Netherlands, France.* John Hopkins Press, 1971.

Studies in Comparative Local Government. 'Citizen Participation and Local Government in Europe.' Winter 1971.

Welfield, Irving H. *European Housing Subsidy Systems.* US Department of Housing and Urban Development, Office of International Affairs, Washington, DC, 1972.

Notes on Contributors

CARLOS M. ALVARADO was head of the Urban Renewal and Housing Corporation (the Puerto Rico Housing Authority) in Puerto Rico from 1960–69. Since then he has been a planning consultant co-ordinating a variety of urban development projects.

JOHN APELROTH serves as Editor of *Beboerbladet Boligen*, a magazine of the Federation of Non Profit Housing in Denmark, as well as the public relations officer of this organization.

TERENCE BENDIXSON was planning correspondent for the *(Manchester) Guardian* from 1962–9. After working for a time for the environment bureau of *The (Sunday) Observer*, he moved to Paris to work in the Urban Division of the Organisation for Economic Co-operation and Development.

SVEN BENGTSON has been a member of the Research Department in the Swedish Confederation of Trade Unions (LO). He is also a member of a study group on housing set up by the Swedish Social Democratic Party. He is now Chief of Research in the National Social Insurance Board.

J. S. FUERST (Editor) was for many years Director of Research and Statistics for the Chicago Housing Authority and is now Assistant Director of Urban Studies at Loyola University, Chicago.

TIBOR GASPAR is a City architect and head of the Town Planning and Design Office in Budapest.

MAURICE LANGLET is Secretary General of the National Federation of HLM Organisations and President of the French Confederation of Housing and Urban Affairs.

YEVGENY SAMODAYEV is a civil engineer and in charge of the Department of Construction for the State Building Committee of the USSR Council of Ministers. He is also a member of the Collegium.

ISRAEL SHAHAM is Assistant Director-General of Budget and Finance, as well as of Programme Planning for the Ministry of Housing, Israel.

JOHANN WOLFGANG WERNER is currently Director of the Executive Committee of Neue Heimat in Hamburg. He also serves on a number of federal committees concerned with housing and urban development.

Index

For Product Safety Concerns and Information please contact our EU
representative GPSR@taylorandfrancis.com
Taylor & Francis Verlag GmbH, Kaufingerstraße 24, 80331 München, Germany